HERBERT FEIS, economist and Pulitzer Prize winner in History, has had a distinguished career as a scholar, a writer, and as an influental adviser to the U. S. government. He was graduated from Harvard in 1916 and took his Ph. D. there in 1921. He taught at Harvard, at the University of Kansas, and from 1926 to 1929 he was head of the Economics Department at the University of Cincinnati. From 1930 to 1931 he was on the staff of the Council of Foreign Relations. In 1931 he began a period of government service, as Adviser on International Economic Affairs to the Department of State (1931-1943), chief technical adviser for the American delegation at the World Economic and Monetary Conference in London (1933), special adviser at the Conference of American Republics (1936, 1938, 1939), Special Consultant to the Secretary of War (1944-47), and member of the State Department's policy planning staff (1950-51). He has been a member of the Institute for Advanced Study and a Guggenheim fellow.

Mr. Feis has written many books, including: *Europe: The World's Banker 1870-1914* (1930); *Seen from E.A.: Three International Episodes* (1946); *The Spanish Story* (1948); *The Road to Pearl Harbor* (1950); *The Diplomacy of the Dollar* (1950); *The China Tangle* (1953); *Churchill-Roosevelt-Stalin* (1957); *Between War and Peace: The Potsdam Conference* (1960); *Japan Subdued* (1961); *Foreign Aid and Foreign Policy* (1964); and *Contest Over Japan* (1967).

THE DIPLOMACY OF THE DOLLAR

1919—1932

HERBERT FEIS

The Norton Library

W · W · NORTON & COMPANY · INC ·

NEW YORK

Books That Live
The Norton imprint on a book means that in the publisher's
estimation it is a book not for a single season but for the years.
W. W. Norton & Company, Inc.

SBN   393   00333-7

PRINTED IN THE UNITED STATES OF AMERICA

3 4 5 6 7 8 9 0

PREFACE

DURING the decade of the twenties, the dollar figured large in our relations with other nations. We acted as banker to the whole needy world. Private capital provided the funds. But the American Government concerned itself with the lending operations. In this essay (originally written as a series of lectures) I have tried to tell how it did, why, and to what effect.

The main words in the title I have chosen, " The Diplomacy of the Dollar," have been, I know, long coupled in the term "dollar diplomacy." So linked, they were used to denote a diplomacy unduly influenced by particular private interests — and given to aid them with too much zeal and favor. Our diplomacy in Central and South America during the years, 1908-12, was warped in this way; and it was then that the name came into vogue. Ever since it has been a term of odium.

But the association between the American dollar and American diplomacy is now of another nature. It is time, therefore, to dissolve the old verbal liaison in favor of a new one — " the diplomacy of the dollar." I offer the name as meaning the way in which we use our power to make gifts or loans to serve our ends in our dealings with other peoples. May the ways be so just and peace-bringing that the name gains in honor fast.

For the assignment assumed the time was short. I sought to convey, interpret, and reflect upon the whole of a large experience — rather than give an exhaustive account of part of it. Here and there I have drawn upon unpublished information. But the main facts which make up the story are to be found in the official series of State Department documents, called *Foreign Relations of the United States*, and in the printed records of the several investigations of our foreign lending made by committees of Congress during the thirties.

The writing of these lectures was made pleasant by the kindness of Johns Hopkins University in asking me to give them; and the task of editing them was made easy by memory of the warm friendliness of the faculty of that University during my stay there. Malcolm Moos and Owen Lattimore were stimulating as well as genial hosts.

I owe thanks to my former colleague, Frederick C. Livesey, for his full and generous instruction to me about the matters of which I have written. I am also greatly obliged to Leland Harrison, who was Assistant Secretary of State during the period under review, to Arthur N. Young, who was Economic Adviser in the State Department during the same period, and to Leroy D. Stinebower and Robert Tufts, my later associates in the State Department, for reviewing the manuscript. Their comments on both facts and interpretation were of much and guiding use. But their willingness to help me tell the story should not be taken to mean that they agree with my version of it.

HERBERT FEIS

The Institute for Advanced Study
    Princeton, New Jersey

CONTENTS

CONTENTS

CHAPTER I

IDEAS, INTERESTS, AND ATTITUDES

1

THE great depression that began in 1929 brought our first great venture in foreign lending to a sick end. There had been a thrill about this swift financial ascension over the oceans. It was gone, and seemingly for all time.

Our former associates in World War I were revolting at the war debt settlements which they felt the American Government had imposed upon them. The fabric of friendship between ourselves and Western Europe was being worn by rubbing over the stones of debt.

Private loans and investments were in the same plight. Promises were being denied or broken; defaults were taking place; losses were being suffered. We were heaping blame on those to whom we had lent or trusted our dollars; and they were heaping blame on us.

A general sigh of resolve was to be heard over the United States: never again should we lend or invest our money in foreign lands. We were about to dismiss the rest of the world as bad company. The bankers were being arraigned by those who had lost their savings as ignorant, shortsighted, and greedy. The Government was being charged with neglect because of the influence of Wall Street in its counsels.

In turn, the foreign world was reproaching us for many of its troubles. The American economic system was being

denounced as unreliable and ruthless; debtors were point-
ing to our high tariffs, the decline in our purchases of
their products, and the abrupt cessation of our loans as
reasons for their failure to pay what they owed.

There was disquieting criticism of another sort about
one particular part of our foreign financial activity—the
loans that had been made to and investments in various
of the small countries of Central America. These were
suspect by many as the wedge or the block—it was never
clear which—of an imperialistic purpose. The American
Government, the charge read, was policing these countries,
and forcing them to submit to control, in order that
bankers might collect and snatch the resources of this
region for themselves. Assertions to that effect, vigorously
expressed in Latin America and the United States, travelled
round the world.

In sum — as a venture in diplomacy, as an attempt to
gain friends and influence nations, the external operations
of American capital seemed to be ending in acid failure.

I still have a copy of the extract from Charles Lamb
which was passed appreciatively from one Government
office to another at the time:

" The human species," this went, " according to the best theory I
can form of it, is composed of two distinct races, the men who borrow,
and the men who lend. . . . The infinite superiority of the former,
which I choose to designate as the great race, is discernible in their
figure, port, and a certain instinctive sovereignty. The latter are born
degraded. ' He shall serve his brethren.' There is something in the
air of one of this cast, lean and suspicious; contrasting with the open,
trusting, generous manners of the other. . . . What a careless, even
deportment hath your borrower! what rosy gills! what a beautiful
reliance on Providence doth he manifest,—taking no more thought
than lilies! What contempt for money,—accounting it (yours and
mine especially) no better than dross! What a liberal confounding
of those pedantic distinctions of meum and tuum! or rather, what a
noble simplification of language (beyond Tooke), resolving these sup-

posed opposites into one clear, intelligible pronoun adjective! What near approaches doth make to the primitive community,—to the extent of one-half of the principle at least! "

When I say that these lines were conned, I mean in the United States of course. Abroad, where debtors read stern demands for payment, feeling found gratified echo in other classic texts—among them the *Merchant of Venice*.

2

Yet with what a lively urge, with what bright hopes we had entered this first era of the diplomacy of the dollar.

For most Americans our participation in the first World War was an arousing experience. It was the first time that their lives and thoughts were touched by events abroad; the first time they made real contact with foreign peoples; while for many bankers and business men it was the first time they made money out of foreign business. The country was swept with an exciting sense of greatness, at playing so decisive a part in the world's affairs. This did not fade out when the war ended. We had won the war. We were ready in our sprouting confidence to take on the next jobs; to clean up the rubble of the war and get the world going again. Europe would be put on its feet. American energy, shrewdness, honesty, skill—and above all else—American dollars would do it. We would, as the thought was then expressed, bring the world back to " normalcy."

To those who had a quick eye there was a glimpse of profit in the prospect. The investment and banking houses had sensed the temper and grasped the chance. Save for a few they were untrained and—it must be said—unfit for the task of guiding the flow of American capital abroad. The more cautious and fastidious — the more responsible among them—were lost in the push. The others went about

arranging loans with an air of "carbonated swagger."[1]
The commsisions to be gained were quick and large, and
the commercial banks willingly financed the business.

Private banking got moral ease for its conduct from the
"central banks" of the large industrial countries — particularly our Federal Reserve System and the Bank of
England. The eminent heads of these institutions, particularly Benjamin Strong of the New York Federal Bank,
and Montagu C. Norman of the Bank of England, were
striving to restore international monetary arrangements
of the sort that had existed before the war. These were
based on the gold standard, the control by banks of credit
and interest rates, and a regulated ebb and flow of liquid
funds between countries. Dollar aid was essential to restore the reserves and stabilize the currencies of many of
the war-struck countries of Europe—if the international
system was ever to function again. Thus the Central
Banks played an active part behind the scenes in arranging
some of the largest loans. And, in passing it may be remarked, that the student of the period gets the impression
that Strong and Norman thought they could manage this
business of international lending better than the governments to which their institutions were attached. This was
their imperium out of which they would have liked to keep
all vulgar intrusion.

To the buyers of foreign bonds and stocks the high
promised rates of return were the great attraction. Bonds
of old, and, it was thought, strong and dependable foreign
governments like those of Holland, France, Belgium,
Italy, and Japan, could be bought at a yield at least half
again greater than any corresponding American bond.

There was still one other economic component in the
urge. During the war the United States had shown a much

[1] The descriptive phrase is Moritz Bonn's.

greater capacity to produce both farm and manufactured products than ever was known. Puzzled doubt stained the surface of our confidence as to where and how we should ever be able to sell what we now knew we could produce. Our exports had grown greatly during the war. If they could be maintained by foreign investment — and wise and respected men ("bankers" and "money doctors" and "money wizards", as the American financial advisers who treated the economic troubles of foreign countries before injecting a loan were then called) said they could be— then American industry and agriculture would be spared hard and costly adjustment. Thus the business community smiled upon the outward movement of capital.

But the urge to finance the world had not come entirely from the youthful heart or the gainful wish. A vague sense of obligation existed—to respond to the deep need and desire of other countries for our aid. The countries on whose side we had fought had suffered great destruction and dislocation. They sought the means to buy food and raw materials, to rebuild bridges, roads, railways, public utilities and to restore their money and banking systems. Alongside of them and in the same plight were the defeated countries, especially Germany. To the north the Dominion of Canada had discovered during the war, like ourselves, the size of its powers. To the south, in the Latin American Republics there was a highly awakened demand for capital for every purpose, private and public. Virtually the whole world claimed, as a matter of justice, support from our greater and uninjured strength.

The American people had been touched by the duty and attracted by the vision. Most were opposed, as the struggle over our entry into the League of Nations showed, to share in the task and risks of organizing the world for peace. But still they were disposed to relieve its suffering, to rebuild its destroyed parts and to help it regain health and strength. They were pleased that their dollars might do these things. They were hopeful that their dollars could do them. And, perhaps, they thought they were excused from doing more by doing that much.

3

The authorities in office in the main shared these sentiments and judgments. They recognized the needs which produced the calls for American aid and were glad to see American private capital respond. It was deemed contrary to good public finance and good public policy that the American Government itself should make foreign loans. As stated by Secretary of State Hughes in August, 1923: "It is not the policy of our Government to make loans to other governments, and the needed capital if it is to be supplied at all, must be furnished by private organizations. . . ."

The prevailing view was that the American citizen should not be taxed and the American Government should not borrow in order to lend abroad; that foreign seekers of capital should go to the private American investor for it; that he could make his decisions and arrange his deals on a paying business basis while the Government could not; and that if the Government began to make loans it would soon find itself entangled in international quarrels and intrigues—against its wish.

The chief officials of all three Administrations that were in office during this era—those of Harding, Coolidge, and Hoover—were of this mind. They were in favor of our foreign financial activity. They believed in the benefits to ourselves and others—of the loans and investments that were being made. They thought it best that in the main the dollar should conduct its own diplomacy, select its own assignments, and make its own terms.

But all three Administrations found they could not leave it entirely alone to do so. For it appeared that not all the projects in which private capital wished to engage would be in the American public interest or consonant with official designs. Some might be used for purposes deemed bad; or enable other governments to ignore our wishes, or obligations to us; or likely to end in default which would cause trouble in or with some foreign land. And presently it appeared also that the chance to grant or deny an American loan was a needed and usable asset in some troubling negotiations.

Thus the Government found itself watching, then asking questions, then commenting, and then advising, for and against. But always with caution and restraint. For it was afraid that it might be smacked for interfering with private affairs and brought to book for mistakes. And it did not like to bargain with or about human welfare; or to subject the working activity of the world to the callous touch of politics. There was a wholesome wish to keep the effort of men to earn a living, or make a career, apart from, clear of, the clashes between nations. For these reasons it stayed behind a screen whence its opinions about loans came like spirit messages; and the collapse found it sitting dazed before an empty lamp.

4

It was in the summer of 1921 that the Government first decided to maintain a watch over the loan offerings made to the American public. The head of the office of Morgan and a few other bankers were asked to come to Washington to discuss the subject with President Harding and the Secretaries of State, Treasury, and Commerce. They then gave a promise (confirmed in a letter of June 6, 1921, from J. P. Morgan and Company to the President) that

American investment bankers would notify the State Department of contemplated transactions, and give it a chance to comment.

Letters between Cabinet members during the next few months give clues to the reasons for this initiative. A difference of accent in regard to the proper purpose and scope of official interest appears between the lines.

The interest of the Secretary of the Treasury, Andrew D. Mellon, derived from the wish to collect the war debts due us from the governments of Europe. In this he was in accord with the insistent will of Congress. Even that early there were signs that the war-stricken nations were unhappy at the thought of having to pay. Mellon wanted to use the chance to grant or deny them access to the American private purse as a means of getting them to do so.

The Secretary of Commerce, Herbert Hoover, was concerned with the same matter but his thoughts had a somewhat different slant. As stated in a letter to Secretary of State Hughes on April 29, 1922:

Another instance of these moral responsibilities lies in loans to countries already indebted to the United States Government in large sums and who from every apparent prospect will not be able to meet these obligations to the American people. Our Federal authorities must have some responsibility in not informing our citizens (or the promoters) that these nations will probably have to confess inability to meet their creditors. Unless some such action is taken the citizens from whom such information has been withheld would seem to me to have the moral right to insist that the Federal Government should not press its governmental claims to the prejudice of their investment.

This reflected Hoover's opinion, often expressed, that the Government ought to alert and guard the private investor against poor loans. He believed it should see that they were fully informed about the situations in which they were asked to provide capital, warned against dubious ventures. And even further, that the Government should try to discourage loans which might be used for war, or produce economic or political instability. But all this he would have sought to do merely by requiring full disclosure of facts (supplemented perhaps by private advice to the bankers and public statements) not by direct exercise of control.

Secretary of State Hughes (and I may interject, Kellogg after him) was chary of assuming so extensive a realm of responsibility. But his concern also scattered broadly. As explained in a note which he sent his colleagues in December, 1921, " a watch," seemed to him, " necessary in order that the Department of State may be in a position better to assist American undertakings abroad and may not be embarrassed in the application of its general policies." [2]

The kind of situations he had in mind can be surmised. The American Government was enmeshed in several troubling disputes in Central America which had originated in, or been made more stubborn by, the accepted need to protect the loans, property, or lives of foreign investors in these countries. We had troops in Haiti, Santo Domingo, Nicaragua, and were quarrelling with Mexico. Hughes wanted to guard against new financial

[2] As more fully stated by Hughes in another letter to Hoover (July 24, 1922), " So far as foreign loans are concerned, the interest of this Department in being consulted arises primarily from its relation to the giving of diplomatic support in the event of future difficulties, and more broadly from the important bearing of these transactions upon the conduct of our foreign relations. For example, I am disposed to discountenance loans to unrecognized governments, or loans sought by foreign governments for military purposes or for objects that appear to run counter to clearly defined policies of this Government." — *Foreign Relations of the United States*, 1922, II, 764-66.

This annual series of volumes will hereinafter be cited as *Foreign Relations*.

operations which might make it harder to manage these situations or create others of the same kind. The American Government was bending its utmost effort to effect a treaty program designed to assure order and peace for China and over the Pacific. Hughes wanted to be sure that all employments of capital in this area were consonant with this great political project.

President Harding added a segment of interest when on January 12, 1922, he wrote the Secretary of State: "I do not suppose there is any way in which we can absolutely control American loans, but I do think our efforts for accomplishment in the way of disarmament ought to justify a request to American bankers that no loans shall be made to any power which is making increased expenditures for armament purposes."

This was the diversity of ideas which led the American Government to enter upon the practice of passing upon American foreign loans and investments. They were left uncodified and flexible, to be further defined as cases came up. The official watch was regarded as a way of warding off interference with a few main American foreign policies rather than a positive exercise of our national power. The officials concerned were guided more by theory and principle — right or wrong — than by strategy. The theory, derived from domestic finance, was that investment was a private business. The principle was that we sought little from the outside world, save that it be peaceful and pay its debts.

5

These thoughts also swayed the Government in its choice of a technique for supervising foreign loans: particularly, to repeat, the wish to give no honest ground for a belief that the loans made had official endorsement and that the Government, therefore, would see that they were paid; and the wish to avoid the charge that it was engaging in a cold and calculated "dollar diplomacy" (which in the milieu of opinion was then identified with "imperialism" or "involvement" or both).

Secretary Hoover was of the opinion that no formula could be found to which "in the more ignorant public mind a certain measure of Government responsibility would not attach." He thought that any controls had better be exercised by the Commerce Department than by the State Department, and without any public announcement, and with the aid of the Executive Committee of the American Bankers Association. But Hughes disagreed and President Harding supported him.

When it turned out that some investment bankers were not keeping the promise that had been given by J. P. Morgan, the Cabinet concluded that firmer action was required. Despite misgiving, it was agreed that all banking groups should be directly and openly told what was expected of them, and that a public explanation should be given of what was being done and why. In March, 1922, the Government announced that all issuers of foreign loans to be sold to the public were being explicitly asked to ascertain the attitude of the State Department in writing before concluding the transaction. The reason given was only a broad affirmation that "the [State] Department believes that in view of the possible national interests involved it should have the opportunity of saying to the underwriters concerned, should it appear advisable to do so, that there is or is not objection to any particular issue." However, the statement went on to make clear, "the Government will not pass upon the merits of foreign loans as business propositions, nor assume any responsibility whatever in connection with loan transactions."

The State Department decided that its comments, made in response to notices of proposed financing received from the bankers, should be as brief and nearly uniform as possible. The form of words adopted was originally, in the cases of those loans that passed scrutiny: "the Department, in the light of the information at hand, offers no objection to the proposed transaction." Or in the contrary case, "the Department is not in a position, therefore to say that there is no objection to the proposed transaction." Or sometimes — "the Department is unable to view the proposed financing with favor at this time."

But as time went on it was found advisable to add to the form of response, to vary it, sometimes to qualify and sometimes to explain. One standard addition soon made was a paragraph calling attention to the fact that the State Department did not pass upon the merits of foreign loans as business propositions nor assume any responsibility in connection with such transactions. Soon also a special form of reply was adopted for use in regard to loans in Germany. Of that I will tell later.

For several years this procedure and these formulas aroused little comment or objection among the public or in banking circles. But gradually criticism spread. Active elements in Congress and in the press asserted that the practice of the State Department was illusory, illegal, and unsound. Senator Glass of Virginia was tireless in repeating this opinion in words that grew more and more angry. He and others charged that, despite all disavowals, the knowledge that the Government had been consulted before a loan was offered for sale was being taken to mean that it was officially approved — both as a business risk and political favor. As the years went on this view spread. The State Department conscientiously denied the inference. But I find it hard to name either officials or students who bluntly took the other side; who spoke up for more, not less, supervision by the Government; or who clamored for a closer liaison between financial, economic, and diplomatic policy. Two pits—the country thought at the time —lay gaping: involvement and imperialism; and it did not want the State Department to get close to the edge of either, lest it fall in.

In banking circles there was some grumbling about the practice, but no active opposition. This may have been because it turned out that the Government did not often stand in the way of a good business deal. In almost all cases where the Government entered an objection, it could be gotten round or in time removed. Still the necessity of consultation, of informing the Department, or waiting for a reply, of sometimes being called upon to give more facts or reasons, and even sometimes of changing loan terms, was a nuisance. The banking houses abided by the procedure. They did not resist it publicly. But they stubbornly contested any real interference with their freedom to do business.

In 1929 Stimson, who had followed Kellogg as Secretary of State, asked the Under Secretary of State, Joseph C. Cotton, to find a way to simplify the practice and to immunize it against misunderstanding, criticism, and abuse. Thereafter, the State Department took to formulating the answers made to bankers pretty much on its own. Commerce was asked merely to supply advisory information on the financial aspects of the transaction. The Treasury, now that the debts due the American Government were funded, accepted a similarly nominal role.

The standard form of answer to the bankers was changed. Instead of being told that the State Department had no objection, they were thereafter told "the Department is not interested." It was thought that this more colorless phrase would make it clearer that the Government was in no way passing on the merits of the loan. But this did not end the criticisms of the practice—which were carried into the Presidential campaign of 1932. The Democrats blamed the Republican Administration for the losses suffered in foreign investment.[3]

[3] Roosevelt (at Columbus, Ohio, August 20, 1932) said that if he were elected he promised that " . . . it will no longer be possible for international bankers or others to sell foreign securities to the investing public of America on the implied understanding that these securities have been passed on or approved by the State Department or any other agency of the Federal Government."

Earlier in this notable speech his caustic version of the economics of recent foreign lending was put in the form of an added fragment to *Alice in Wonderland.*

" A puzzled, somewhat skeptical Alice asked the Republican leadership some simple questions:

" ' Will not the printing and selling of more stocks and bonds, the building of new plants and the increase of efficiency produce more goods than we can buy? '

" ' No,' shouted Humpty Dumpty. ' The more we produce the more we can buy.'

" ' What if we produce a surplus? '

" ' Oh, we can sell it to foreign consumers.'

" ' How can the foreigners pay for it? '

" ' Why, we will lend them the money.'

" ' I see,' said little Alice, ' they will buy our surplus with our money. Of course, these foreigners will pay us back by selling us their goods? '

" ' Oh, not at all,' said Humpty Dumpty. ' We set up a high wall called the tariff.'

" ' And,' said Alice at last, ' how will the foreigners pay off these loans? '

" ' That is easy,' said Humpty Dumpty, ' did you ever hear of a moratorium? '

" And so, at last, my friends, we have reached the heart of the magic formula of 1928. . . . "

6

In this fashion, then, the Government put itself in a position where it could have imposed on the outward movement of American capital the stamp of its ideas and authority. But for the most part the stamp was lightly and sparingly applied.

This policy accorded with a sincere belief that the forces of economic growth — represented by this capital movement — could find a path through almost any political situation, and bring benefit both to the recipients and ourselves. And with some the belief ran even further: that the economic improvement brought about by the investment would be a cure for the political troubles; that if all nations became prosperous they would settle their quarrels, cease to fear and envy one another, and live in peace.

Thus, in a sense, our foreign lending was regarded as part of our contribution to the contemporary effort to improve relations between nations. A contribution which conformed to the rest of our foreign policy for it left us outside of all alignments and free of all obligations; but still it showed we were not indifferent to the condition of foreign nations.

The impression now prevailing, that during the twenties our foreign policy was wholly negative, is wrong. The American Government exerted itself most earnestly to create a treaty basis of law and order in all parts of the world. With diligence it advocated treaties of conciliation and arbitration. It was the main mover of the important Nine Power Pact of 1922, for the stabilization of the situation in the Far East. It, along with the French Government, brought about the Pact of Paris (the so-called Kellogg-Briand Pact) in which all the participants renounced war as an instrument of national policy. This was, in the United States, an era of faith in exchange of vows and promises between governments, even when the pledges were unclear, qualified, and no recourse was provided against those who twisted or broke them. Such was the line of aspiration and effort. And just as now it is felt that the bridge between desire and achievement would be some form of accord on the production and use of atomic energy, so then it was thought to be an agreement for the limitation and reduction of armaments. The American Government made a devout effort to bring this about. The whole policy, it need hardly be said, was swamped by events.

That can be regarded as a tragedy of good and unselfish intentions. Not so the course we followed in our foreign economic relations—which was selfish as well as lax, and less excusable. We sought and rejoiced in the expansion of our foreign trade. But we refused to face the fact that it lacked a healthy balance; and that it was being sustained by loans that would in the end be too great a burden upon foreign debtors. We maintained high tariffs. We tenaciously claimed repayment of war debts which prejudiced prospects of solvency of the private investment which we were encouraging. Internally we permitted a growth of speculation and of credit expansion which finally ended in the collapse of 1929.

These features in our foreign political and foreign economic policy condemned our diplomacy of the dollar to be rambling and fumbling; and it turned out to be a well meant, but thorough muddle.

What we tried to accomplish, and how, is best told by reviewing—as I will in the next section—the instances in which the American Government intervened. These, when listed, seem numerous and diverse. Therefore, do not forget that they are scattered through a decade; that at the time the Government thought that occasional correction and support was all that was needed; that success in fact was in sight; that the world outside us—with the help of the dollar—was on its way towards a secure and prosperous future.

CHAPTER II

THE EFFORT OF GOVERNMENT TO GUIDE INVESTMENT

1

HOOVER, then Secretary of Commerce, in 1927 mused before the Third Pan-American Commercial Conference, " . . . if nations would do away with the lending of money for the balancing of budgets, for purposes of military equipment or war, or even that type of public works which do not bring some direct or indirect public return, a great number of blessings would follow to the entire world."

The same thoughts roamed through the State Department—before and during Hoover's term of office. They turned up often in the notations which were made on letters of notice received from bankers. They loitered in the only systematic statement of the rules for the guidance of loan operations to be found in the files—a note prepared by the Undersecretary of State Joseph Cotton in July, 1929, just as the era of foreign lending was verging towards its end.

This was a summary for use within the Government of "the five classes of objectionable loans as to which adverse action may be considered." They were:

1) Loans to governments for balancing of budgets as a result of insufficient taxation;

2) Loans for military purposes;

3) Loans for assistance to foreign monopolies where their conduct is such as to maintain prices against the American consumer;

4) Loans to governments not recognized by the United States;

5) Loans to governments or citizens in countries who have failed to maintain their obligations to the United States.

But these injunctions about the kinds of financing deemed desirable, and those deemed not, were not really tested or effectively applied. In practice they fared this way:

1. *Loans to meet budget deficits.*—A sizable fraction of the loans obtained by foreign governments were used to pay expenses that might have been foregone or met by current taxes, without acute deprivation. But most of the borrowing was justified by use and by wont. The amounts loaned to foreign industries, public utilities, banks, etc., and the direct investment in enterprises of which Americans secured direct control exceeded our loans to governments. In the main the proceeds of the American lending were used productively, i. e., to support or stimulate useful work or increase its yield.

2. *Loans for armaments.*—The borrowers and bankers were seldom naive enough to place before the State Department a loan prospectus which stated that the proceeds were for armaments or other military expenses. But many of the loans allowed by the State Department were for countries which simultaneously were spending much "for military purposes." Had American capital not been provided, these countries would either have had to live more poorly or spend less on arms. However, in retrospect, the amount of dollars they devoted to maintaining their military forces seems small; and later we had cause to regret that the Western democracies were more saving in that respect than the countries that formed the Axis.

3. *Loans for foreign monopolies.*—Here the Government had in mind primarily schemes to control supplies of raw materials imported by the United States. In a few conspicuous cases the organizers of such monopolies, denied loans in the United States, found a way to get the wanted financing somewhere else. But it is probable that the official ban discouraged other ventures of the same kind. In the industrial field, many foreign enterprises that were parties to restrictive accords borrowed here.

4. *Loans to governments not recognized by us.*—This ban was effectively maintained. But in most instances the governments who were refused American capital managed to survive without it.

5. *Loans to governments in default to American Government.*—This rule was rigorously applied.

This general estimate does not tell enough of what occurred or why. More is to be learned by unwinding the tight tape of classification.

2

Of all the uses made of official influence, the most consistent was for the purpose of collecting war debts.

The American Government, in effect, made it impossible for the public authorities and private enterprises in France, Belgium, Italy, Greece, Roumania and Yugoslavia to borrow in the United States until the governments of these countries settled their accounts with the American Treasury.

Among the owing countries, France held back most stubbornly. Five years after the end of the war French popular opinion and the French Government were still averse to giving the American Government an unqualified promise to pay. This reluctance extended even to the remittance of some $400 million which the French Government owed for surplus Army war material bought from us after the end of the war. Further, the French Government was opposed to granting to the United States the small share of German annuities (under the Dawes Plan) which we sought as payment of cost for the Army of Occupation and war damage claims.

Then in November, 1924, the French Government besought, through the Morgan firm which had advanced it large sums, a big dollar loan—of private investors and at good interest. The American Government advised the bankers and the French that it would not look with favor on the issuance of this loan.[1] The French Government thereupon yielded on some points. Payments from accumulated reparations receipts on our claims equal to those made to our allies were obtained, as well as an allocation of a small fraction of future annuities. A settlement was also reached in regard to a scheme of payment for Army supplies.[2] The American Government thereupon suspended its objection and the loan was issued and sold with a flourish.

But not long afterwards the French resistance (to paying the war debt) raided the position of our Treasury more boldly. In "the balance sheet of France" which the French Minister of Finance, Clementel, presented to the Chamber of Deputies in the following December there was no item of war debt to Britain or the United States. In explanation of this he said "strict justice would seem

[1] See the telegram from the Secretary of State to the American Ambassador in France (Herrick), November 11, 1924. — *Foreign Relations*, 1924, II, 72.

[2] The settlement was formally expressed in the Final Protocol of the Conference [of Finance Ministers] and Agreement regarding the Distribution of the Dawes Annuities, signed at Paris, January 14, 1925. — *Ibid.*, 1925, II, 145, *et seq*.

to demand a general pooling of war expenditures and their allotment among Allied States proportionately to the riches of each one. . . ."[3] When one of the Deputies, Louis Marin, expanded the same disturbing doctrine, almost the whole Chamber rose to applaud. "While war still raged," he said, "statesmen in every country appealed to the common cause. Some gave their ships, some munitions, some the lives of their sons, some money, and today only those who gave money come saying to us: 'Give back what we loaned.'"

Shortly thereafter the ban was imposed again. The State Department let it be known that it would not look with favor upon any further French financing until the French Government settled its debt. It held to this position consistently in its answers to the many banking groups that wanted to issue bonds for the French Government, French cities, railways, steamship lines, public utilities, factories, and hotels. Again the penalty was effective.

In September, 1925, the French Government sent a debt delegation to the United States to negotiate with the American World War Foreign Debt Commission. But agreement could not be reached on a permanent funding plan. We proposed a temporary arrangement for five years during which France was to pay a small annual sum. Even this the French Cabinet refused to approve. The State Department spread a reminder through the press that neither the French Government nor French industry would be able to borrow in the United States unless the arrangement was approved.

[3] *Inventaire de la situation financière de la France au début de la treizième législature, presenté par M. Clementel, ministre des finances* (Paris, 1924). Clementel thought that the American Government misinterpreted his remarks and his purposes. See telegram from Herrick to the Secretary of State, December 31, 1924. — *Ibid.*, 1925, I, 137.

The French renewed negotiations. In April, 1926, a permanent settlement was signed. But no French Cabinet dared to submit it for ratification to the Chamber of Deputies. During that year France was having monetary trouble, the value of the franc declined sharply. There was a wish to borrow here in order to arrest the fall and stabilize the franc. But since we maintained the ban, the French had to manage without the usual American public loan. They did. The franc rebounded in value; it was successfully stabilized; the gold and foreign exchange reserves of the Bank of France rose fast.

Unpoliced or indirect ways of borrowing dollars were used instead of the public borrowing operations which came within the purview of the State Department. Short-term credits were arranged with New York banks. Loans were floated in Holland, Switzerland, and Sweden. Some bond issues, payable in dollars, were also sold in Canada and American investors bought them there. The Swedish Match Company, Kreuger's strange creation, lent large sums to the French Government; soon after its American subsidiary (the International Match Company) sold $50 million worth of its own bonds in the United States. The student of these times may well marvel at the extent to which the world then financed itself by selling bonds guaranteed by anticipated profits from the sale of matches. The matches were scratched but the bonds went up in smoke.

However that may be, at the end of 1927 the State Department concluded that it was no longer worth while to continue to obstruct French financing. Our relations with France were, it began to feel, being hurt; while the chances of inducing France to ratify the Debt Agreement were being prejudiced rather than improved. But the Treasury differed. Payment for surplus Army stocks was soon to come due; and the Treasury thought the French Government might have to borrow in the United States to meet this payment, unless, alternatively, it ratified the general debt settlement in which this item would be merged. State and Treasury compromised. The ban was lifted on loans to French industry, maintained a while longer on loans for the French Government.

A few words will complete the story. In July, 1929, the French Government, despite anguished outcry in the Chamber of Deputies, ratified the War Debt Agreement. A flare of amity, lit by the final coming into effect at almost the same time of the Kellogg-Briand Pact, made it easier for the French Government to take this step. The fact that payment in full of the $400 million owed us for war materials was due in a week, may also have influenced this final action. The French Treasury did not want to remit this large sum, and the American Treasury did not want to receive it just then—fearing the effect on the European exchange position.

Thereafter the American capital market was freely open to the French Government. But it did not need to borrow right away; and during the thirties under the crawling fear of both social revolution and war, the movement of capital was the other way: French gold and other liquid resources drained into the United States. I might add that private American buyers of the French securities issued during the twenties — by and large, and over the long term — secured an excellent return in interest and principal.

A similar policy was applied in regard to borrowing by Italy, Belgium, Czechoslovakia, Yugoslavia, and Greece. Objection was maintained until the governments of these countries signed settlements for their war debts. Presently they all did so. Then in short order they borrowed more

than enough dollars to pay the first few small annuities
due to the American Government under the debt settlements. The Italian schedule will serve to illustrate how
close the connection between the will to settle old debts
and the wish to contract new ones; on September 1, 1925,
the State Department said it would not view with favor
the loan which Mussolini's Finance Minister, Volpi, had
negotiated with the Morgan firm; on November 14th a
debt settlement was reached with the American Treasury;
on November 18th the loan contract was signed; and on
the 23rd the State Department said it had no objection
to the issuance of the loan.

Our policy of preventing new borrowing by resistant
debtors was precursor to the Johnson Act. That law, in
force during the thirties, shut the American loan market
to governments in default on the payments they had been
induced to promise in order to open our purse. We beat
that bush until not only the fruit but the leaves were off
the branches. The American Government was forced to
accept the fact that money lent to allies for war or the
repair of war damage was gone. It was spent and not
invested. Isolationists like Senators Johnson and Borah
thought that when that was clear Americans would be so
angry that they would never take sides in any struggle
between foreign nations again. They were wrong.

3

In the Caribbean region the Government tried to be not
only the guardian of American lenders but also friend and
tutor of the local small republics. Hence, it played a far
more active part in determining what American loans and
investments were made in this region than anywhere else.[4]

[4] The volumes of *Foreign Relations* during the pertinent years give
the record of official activity in regard to the financing of this area.

The thoughts which guided the State Department were benign, though there were few south of the Rio Grande who thought so. The problem was well exposed in a speech by Hughes to the American Bar Association in August, 1923. It summed up to this: that the troubles of these small republics were in no small measure due to their poverty and to the lack of development of their resources; that capital was needed for progress; that it was not the policy of the American Government to make loans; that private capital would only be obtainable if the investment was reasonably secure and the profit commensurate with the risk. Therefore, the American Government was impelled to use its influence to work out arrangements to provide security for loans which otherwise would be denied, while also preventing unfairness and imposition. "We are not seeking," Hughes affirmed in conclusion, "to extend this relation but to limit it; we are aiming not to exploit but to aid; not to subvert, but to help in laying the foundations for sound, stable, and independent government."

This is essentially true of the policy pursued by the American Government during the twenties. But the interpretation fails to take due account of the fact that the private interests concerned did not fully share this viewpoint or desire. They usually wanted as much protection and profit as could be had—whether or not freedom was lost in the process. And sometimes they could find local political partners equally indifferent to the point. The State Department could not dictate the decisions of either, and did not find it easy to keep a fair balance between the claims of lenders and the claims of freedom.

A good explanation and defense of these policies is to be found in the speech of the Economic Adviser of the State Department, Arthur N. Young, at the Institute of Politics, Williamstown, Massachusetts.

Still, taking the decade as a whole, the Government was roughly successful in its purposes. Bondholders were paid and (with the exception of the oil companies in Mexico) American property investments prospered. Washington persuaded bankers to yield more, and caused them to reduce their demands for control and security. It helped the Central American states to get and keep solvent; it curbed graft; and it taught them to manage their financial and monetary affairs better. In these ways our official guardianship benefited the smaller republics in the south— enabling them to secure financing that otherwise would not have been made, or on easier terms.

But it was in some situations too severe, and in others too lax. Control over local revenues and expenditures by American financial representatives was at times marked by excessive concern with the interest of the lenders. Local wishes were at times too severely repressed. Not a few of the loan contracts signed during this period yielded the vendors too great a " spread " or profit. Furthermore, careless and dishonest use of loan proceeds was not wholly avoided. Thus, for example, bankers, bondholders and contractors provided funds to the Machado régime in Cuba for a corrupted program of public works, and poured far too many millions into Cuban sugar.[5] But it must be recalled that the State Department insisted that it could and would not pass on questions of business risk. Also, it usually could not, even had it so wished, directly supervise the use of the proceeds by borrowers.

Under treaties, the governments of Cuba, Haiti, and the Dominican Republic were obligated to secure the

[5] The Cuban Government in this case asked for lenders, got them, and accepted a loan bid from the Chase Bank before the State Department made up its mind as to whether or not to object to the financing. The consent was reluctant. — *Foreign Relations*, 1928, II, 640-54.

consent of the American Government to new borrowing. This authority was exercised with good purpose and with some result.

The State Department tried to make sure that before the Mortgage Bank of Panama was financed its operations were protected against corrupt politics. The bank borrowed in Canada instead. It tried to make sure that if the Panamanian Government borrowed for roads, the roads would be well built.[6] This was resented as interference with local independence.

The State Department stopped what it deemed to be improper exploitation schemes which American groups worked out with the governments of Guatemala and Honduras. And when, in 1922, the Orellana Government in Guatemala sought a loan on the basis of a dubious plan for currency and banking reform, the Department objected to both the Guatemalan authorities and the bankers. As the price of consent it sought more thoroughgoing reform, and it expressed dislike for the fact that the bankers would get control of Guatemalan currency and exchange for twenty-seven years. The business was dropped.[7]

Neither aspect of the official policy was popular either in the United States or Latin America. American opinion did not appreciate the real chance that disorder and tyranny might become chronic in this region; nor perceive that its economic and political ways were improving under our tutelage. Many Americans disliked what they construed to be the use of our authority to make a safe field for investment; and were not convinced that the State Department was really trying to avoid intervention. While

[6] *Ibid.*, 1923, II, 687-95.

[7] So also, for further example, see the State Department's objection to the contract signed (February 20, 1922) for the sale of the National Bank of Haiti to the National City Bank. — *Ibid.*, 1922, II, 523, *et seq.*

locally our interference and control was resented by most — by none as much as those whose chances of quick personal gain were spoiled.

Thus the State Department carried on under a pall of suspicious criticism. In April, 1925, President Coolidge, in speaking to the United Press, made a statement that was taken to confirm the suspicion. "The person and property," he said, "of a citizen are a part of the general domain of the nation, even when abroad. . . . There is a distinct and binding obligation on the part of self-respecting governments to afford protection to the persons and property of their citizens, wherever they may be.[8]

This — perhaps wrongly — was taken to mean that the Government would use pressure or even force to assure payment on private loans, particularly in Central America. The press and Congress dissented from the doctrine. They did not want the Government to get more enmeshed in the affairs of the small countries to the south, and more disliked. The State Department took note. Thereafter it was more loath to become involved in local debt and financial situations, even when the reasons were adequate.

During the next few years the Government, responsive to the sense of the country, gradually revised its way of dealing with Central American situations. The unappreciated paternalism waned. The State Department yielded to the demand that American financial supervision be brought to an end — even though local mismanagement followed. A search began for a new and more equal basis of relationship in which economic questions got less attention. If the area was to qualify itself for private American capital, it would henceforth do so by its free choice.

---

[8] This statement, I am informed, was a surprise to those officials in the State Department who were engaged in the day by day business of deciding what protection to give to American private interests in foreign lands.

4

I turn to another segment of official purpose; the wish that American capital should not pay for foreign armament or war. This was narrowly construed, and even so evaded. Borrowers never explicitly asked for dollars to buy arms or support armies. They sought loans for other purposes, and paid their military expenditures out of other funds. The American Government did not question this practice. Nor could it have without seeming to dictate the political and military policies of all borrowers. Or alternatively refusing to permit American capital to go abroad at all.

In a few instances where it was known in advance that some loan was wanted to pay a bill due for arms ordered, the State Department objected. But even in these cases, it was outwitted. Thus, when in October, 1924, the Peruvian Government was arranging to borrow in order to pay for four destroyers which it had bought, the State Department told the bankers that it was not in favor of the loan. This financing, it explained, would make a bad impression in Chile; and should certainly be postponed until the disputes between Peru and Chile over their boundary was settled. The loan was dropped. But the American builder of these destroyers accepted payment over a stretch of years for two of the four, and then later for the other two.[9]

The next year in 1925, the same question was presented when Argentina besought a short-term credit from J. P. Morgan and Company to pay for military equipment

[9] The full circle of irony is illustrated by the action of the War Department in 1930, which sold equipment for twelve Corsair planes to the United Aircraft Company, so that the planes might be sold to the Peruvian Government, so that the American aircraft industry should not be adversely affected.

which it had already ordered abroad. This time the Department said that since there would be no public issue of securities it would not object.

In 1927, the Bolivian Government contracted a large loan in the United States. Later it was learned that part of the proceeds were diverted from the announced purpose to pay a British armament company, the Vickers Armstrong Company, for arms already bought. The American Government was irritated. But in 1928 it made no objection when Bolivia issued a refunding loan which included an item of some $5 million to pay Vickers Armstrong the rest of what Bolivia owed it.

All in all, I think the result of the official attitude in this matter may be summed up this way: it did to some extent influence the flow of American capital away from military and toward civilian purposes; it prevented some small countries from squandering more on arms. But it did not significantly affect the state of armaments, and it did not prevent American capital from providing future aggressors—Germany, Japan, and Italy—with the industrial base for their military program.

5

Another purpose on the Government list was to deter American capital from aiding foreign interests in the exercise of monopolistic control over products we needed to import. Thus, in 1925, it objected to loans wanted by the Coffee Institute of Brazil and the State of Sao Paulo to enable them to store coffee and keep it off the market.[10] The necessary funds were found in London. About a decade later—it may be remarked at the risk of being too fond of paradox—the American Government was to take

[10] *Foreign Relations*, 1925, I, 533-35.

the lead in encouraging the coffee-producing states of Central and South America to agree upon a scheme for dividing up the American market and establishing a system of quotas to maintain the price of coffee.

In 1925 the French-German cartel which had been established to control the export of potash and to divide the American market wanted to raise capital in this country. The State Department prevented it. But one of the participants in the cartel, the Solvay Company, a subsidiary of the Allied Chemical and Dye Company, was permitted to secure some funds here; and again London provided the cartel with the financing it could not raise in New York.[11]

Still again the effort should not be judged as completely futile. Our policy made it harder for foreign monopolies to get capital and made its cost greater.

6

As regards the wish to prevent profligate borrowing that would merely make it easier for foreign governments to have a deficit, I have already commented. The attempt to make it effective was earnest. But it was usually found impractical. Some of the largest loans of foreign governments issued in the United States were specifically intended to enable the foreign governments to meet some current expense for which they might well have taxed their own people. The incisive fact was that in the absence of *permanent* control over the public financing of the borrower, future deficits, deficits *after* the loan was procured, could not be prevented.

Still, if the depression had not come, if old political

[11] The correspondence with the bankers is in *Foreign Relations*, 1926, II, 205-213.

struggles had not re-emerged in Europe, the era of deficits
might have ended.

7

Trivial though the incident was, this account of the
part played by the American Government in guiding the
flow of American capital abroad should not omit one
example of diversity.

In 1925 the Pilsner Brewery of Czechslovakia proposed
to sell bonds in the United States. The State Department
frowned. In the days of constitutional prohibition, it
would have been hard to let the transaction pass. Hence,
the bankers were informed that the transaction was "of
doubtful propriety in view of the spirit of the existing law."

So it turned out that we financed the great steel and
aluminum factories of Germany, and that we provided
the means for reconstructing the Italian shipyards that
built the cruisers that had to be met at Taranto. But we
abstained from providing new vats for Pilsner beer. Perhaps the panjandrums of historical theory, like Marx or
Toynbee, have an easy explanation of this. But the rest
of us can only conclude that Puck was roaming through
the corridors of history in that decade.

8

I have reserved for somewhat longer comment an account of the Government's attempt to influence the dealings of American capital with Japan, Germany, and the
Soviet Union.

The scrutiny over loans to Japan took the American
Government into a sensitized field of foreign policy, touch-
ing our relations with both Japan and China and the
struggle between them. Despite its wish, or in a sense

because of its wish, not to be drawn into that dispute, the Government found that it had to take cognizance of the attempts of Japan to borrow here.

The problem was posed for the first time in 1922, when the Oriental Development Company arranged to have the National City Company underwrite a $20 million loan, to be guaranteed by the Japanese Government. This company had been organized to colonize and exploit Korea. But it operated also in Manchuria, North China, and was beginning to extend its activities to Mongolia and the South Sea Islands. It was controlled by, and in the main financed by, the Japanese Government. The State Department was not enthusiastic about the idea of having American capital make it easier for Japan, which was busily trying to close the "open-door" in Manchuria, to expand its economic control in the other named parts of Asia. Therefore, it told the National City Company that it would rather not see this loan issued, explaining that it might create prejudicial competition with American business in countries outside Japan.

Neither the banking house nor the Japanese Government found this objection insuperable. In January, 1923, the National City Company brought to the Department a message from the Japanese Minister of Finance which said that "to all practical purposes the money would be spent either in Japan or its colonies." When the then head of the Company, Mitchell, called on Hughes to transmit this word, he added that if the State Department continued to object he would have to explain to the Japanese Government the real reason why the bank could not go forward with the transaction. He also laid stress on the fact that similar loans had been arranged in France and Great Britain. At about the same time the American Ambassador in Japan advocated by cable that the State

Department should let the issue pass. But since it was not certain as to where this capital was going to be used, the State Department maintained the objection. A little later, Mitchell served notice that the money would be raised within Japan and that a delicate international situation would be created. Still Hughes did not change his position, and the particular loan was issued within Japan.

Undaunted, the National City Company appeared again — this time with a prospectus which specified that the Oriental Development Company would use what it borrowed here only in Korea and for the redemption of debentures and bank loans. To this the State Department made no objection and the loan was issued in February, 1923.[12] The Oriental Development Company soon started new ventures to the south.

At about the same time, the South Manchurian Railway also wanted to sell a dollar bond issue here. The borrowed funds, the same bankers advised the State Department, would be spent partly in the United States, partly in Manchuria. But, even so, the proposal was adversely judged. The American Government did not like the idea of assisting the South Manchurian Railway to extend the area of its colonization in Manchuria, and thereby to entrench Japan more firmly in that country. Therefore, it advised the National City Company that this was not a desirable transaction; and it repeated the advice in June 1923, when the bankers tried to overcome the objection by proposing that all of the loan should be spent in the United States. This particular bond issue was never floated. But the Japanese Government provided the South Manchurian Railway with the funds it needed. In part,

[12] The correspondence between the State Department and the bankers is given in *Foreign Relations*, 1923, II, 503-9.

these came from the allowed borrowing of the Oriental Development Company.

The next series of Japanese loans in the United States was made by electric public utilities, municipalities, and cities. These the State Department permitted without comment. Then also, in February, 1924, it made no objection to a $150 million loan to the Imperial Japanese Government, mainly used to repair earthquake damage. In July of the same year the Industrial Bank of Japan, another Government institution, managed to borrow $25 million. The information sent by the bankers to the State Department was that this sum also was to be used for reconstruction, but part was diverted.

In 1927 the South Manchurian Railway again sought a loan, and again with the guarantee of the Japanese Government. American investors were by this time showing themselves a little shy about buying Japanese bonds. Moody's Investors Service, then the most respected of its kind, set out to reassure them (in a letter, June, 1927):

" It is, of course, possible that the setback in [Japanese] industrial issues was helped by the belief on the part of a few that there exists the possibility of conflict between our country and Japan. That such fears, if they do exist, are absolutely groundless, a sober analysis will readily show."

This South Manchurian Railway loan was discussed in the Cabinet (about March 25th). President Coolidge was still inclined to allow any borrowing which the Japanese Government might want to do in its own name. But he was still doubtful about the desirability of loans to the South Manchurian Railway. They might, he feared, imply that the Government accepted Japan's claim to a special position in Manchuria.

Morgan and Company were working with the National City Company on the deal. In October, Lamont of the

Morgan firm went to Japan and upon his return put the issue squarely up to the State Department. It wriggled unhappily. It did not wish to offend Japan, but neither did it want to be dragged into the quarrel between Japan and China. On November 23rd, the Chinese Government transmitted to the State Department a protest of Chinese financiers and business men. Still, on the 27th, Secretary of State Kellogg let the press know that he thought that this was a private matter and that the State Department was not particularly interested in it. But three days later Chang Tso-lin, the War Lord of Manchuria, announced that he would consider the loan as a provocative act, and that the Chinese people would hold us responsible; and on December 4th the Chinese Foreign Minister officially protested. Japanese purposes in Manchuria, he asserted to Kellogg, were basically imperialist and the South Manchurian Railway, " a symbol and instrument of alien domination over a large and rich portion of Chinese territory." Both the American Chargé d'Affaires in Peking and the Commander in Chief of our Asiatic Fleet advised Washington that the immediate reaction all over China would be unfavorable.[13]

The State Department let the press get the impression that the loan project would not be broached under the circumstances, that the bankers would decide to drop it. The signal was passed to the bankers; they were told that the State Department thought that the publicity had adversely affected the market for the loan. The Japanese Government could hardly take offense at this report of fact. The bankers agreed. They postponed the issue indefinitely.

[13] The messages between the State Department and its diplomatic missions in the Far East are printed in *Foreign Relations*, 1927, II, 482-92.

But the Japanese Government found it could still secure American capital through other routes. In September, 1928, the Oriental Development Company sold another bond issue in the United States without objection from the State Department. In May, 1930, so did the Japanese Imperial Government.

During this period, it should be borne in mind, the Japanese Government was a party to treaties which pledged all countries with interests in the Pacific to respect the integrity of China and settle all problems that might arise in the area by peaceful means. Its diplomacy was in the main conciliatory. The American Government preferred to allow Japan to grow stronger in the hope that it would grow friendlier—rather than give it another grievance. This turned out in the light of later circumstance to be a mistake. But again, who knows whether it would have been if the depression had not occurred and if our diplomacy had been more decisive.

The dilemma in which the American Government found itself in regard to the financing of Japan is a recurrent one. Within the next few years we shall have to decide anew what countries of the Far East to support with dollars: Japan, China, Korea, Indonesia, India — some or all of them. Will it be China this time that we feel we have to fear, Japan on whom we feel we can rely to be peaceful? Or will there be some new Pacific treaty more clinching than the pact of 1922? These questions are easier to ask than to answer. Our habits have changed; during this first era we thought it enough to take an occasional quick glance at the dial of politics; now we have become alert and confirmed watchers; and it is essential that we be so.

CHAPTER III

SOME SPECIAL EXPERIENCES

1

AMERICAN buyers of German securities financed the recovery of Republican Germany, the repair of the German monetary and banking system, and the payment of German reparations during the twenties. Some one hundred and eighty German bond and stock issues—many of large size—were sold in the United States. The public bought in all almost one and a half billion of German obligations—nominal amount. American banks, as well, made large advances to German (and Austrian and Hungarian) institutions, thinking to be paid off out of later public issues. But the market broke before they were, and in the banking crisis of 1933 some of the largest American banks found themselves with frozen loans in this region to an amount in excess of their total capital.

The State Department warned against and tried to restrain this extension of credit. But the ground on which it stood was narrow and shallow. It did not object to the fact that German strength was being restored. On the contrary, it welcomed the vigorous German recovery. Europe needed German products. We wanted German trade. Our former allies wanted reparations payments and we wanted debt payments from our former allies. The concern of the Government originated in the fear that the debts to American private lenders might conflict with the claims of foreign governments for reparations. Soon, however, it became bothered also by knowledge that the borrowing was excessive, and some of it was for dubious purposes. When the State Department tried to impress the lenders with these points however, they found the bankers unready to forego big profits and the bond buyers unready to ignore high interest rates. The State Department did not press its objections to the point of strain.

The gate was widely opened with the issuance in October 1924, of the so-called Dawes Loan — one of the features of a revised program for reparations payments which had been worked out under tension. This loan was in the total of $200 million of which the American quota was $110 millions. Much of it was intended to support German currency, stabilized after a period of wrecking inflation. As Keynes pointed out at the time, this loan was not a necessary part of the experts' scheme, either economically or financially. The start of the reparations payments could have been postponed; after all the funds provided by this borrowing were only enough to cover the reparations payments Germany had to make during the following eight months. But the loan was an important aid to the restoration of confidence in German currency, and essential to get French and German assent to the experts' plan for the adjustment of reparations.

Morgan and Company were asked by the British and French Governments to sponsor the American share of this loan. They were not jubilant. Almost uniquely in the banking community, they saw the essential point. When, on September 18, 1924, one of the Morgan partners, Dwight Morrow, went to Washington to consult Secretary Hughes, he read a cable from his partners in Paris, Morgan and Lamont. Parts of it retain interest. The Montagu Norman mentioned was Governor of the Bank of England. His influence upon the attitude both of the American banking community and of the British Government towards Germany lasted through almost two decades:

" ' Whole question turns on the actual desire for peace on the part of Germany. Have been very much disturbed by the attitude of the Nationalists in that country who sold their objections to the carrying out of the Dawes Report for a statement to be made by their Government repudiating the war guilt clause in the Treaty of Versailles. So far German Government has not published this repudiation, but of course we cannot be sure that it will not do so. As against this Montagu Norman is quite certain (and he has seen Schacht quite a little) that apart from the Communists on one side and the Nationalists on the other, in Germany the great masses of the people want peace and are ready to make the necessary sacrifices to get it. On the whole the great class of moderate people in any country are the people who rule it.

' Montagu Norman advances many other arguments; most of them may be summed up in the statement that he has honest belief that the Germans intend to meet this loan and the conditions of the Dawes Report honorably. Further, that the Germans will want a great deal more money than the contemplated loan, all of which will be subsequent to that loan and to the total reparations payments. But our loan will be a first charge on everything the country has and the country is subjected to foreign control to an extent that has never yet been accomplished in dealing with any nation; in fact, he believes there is no foreign loan at present in existence which offers as good security as this one.

' Montagu Norman was perfectly clear that in his opinion unless the loan is made Europe will break. If, on the contrary, it is made he believes that the results will be as favorable as those of similar operations for Austria and Hungary have turned out, but on an even larger scale.

*   *   *   *   *   *

What really impresses us favorably in Governor Norman's opinion is not the extent of the foreign control upon Germany but the disposition of the German people at the present time. We have some fear, however, that that disposition may not continue. However desirous Germany is of getting the loan at the moment in order to free the hold which France has upon the industries of the Ruhr, it is almost inevitable that this loan will be unpopular in Germany after a few years. The People of Germany, in our opinion, are almost certain, after sufficient time has elapsed, to think not of the release of the Ruhr but of the extent to which what was once a first-class power has been subjected to foreign control."

Part of the answer which Secretary Hughes gave to the Morgan firm on September 19th will revive memory of our attitude at the time:

> I believe that in all countries the great mass of people want peace. I do not think that the people of Germany constitute an exception. . . . I believe that the execution of the Dawes Plan is necessary. . . . If it failed because American bankers would not aid, I think it would be most unfortunate. In the event of its failure, we should have, in my judgment, not only chaotic conditions abroad but a feeling of deep despair. . . .
>
> Of course I have no right to pledge, and do not attempt to pledge this Government either legally or morally in this matter, and American bankers must act on their own judgment as to the urgency and security. . . . We had hoped that while this Government could not make a loan or give any guarantee, the American financiers would see their way clear to undertake the participation which the world expects and which is believed to be essential to the success of the loan.[1]

American subscriptions to this loan were in excess of $1 billion, about ten times the amount of bonds offered for sale. The banks had to make allotments among the eager applicants. The decline of trust in the international financial outlook since then is shown by the contrast between this response to the Dawes Loan offering and the

[1] As early as June the American Government had been advised by the British Government that the success of the revised plan of reparations, produced by the Committee of Experts of which General Dawes was Chairman, was deemed to depend on an American loan. Hughes had made clear that the American Government did not accept responsibility for the loan. But he had instructed our Ambassador in London (Kellogg) to use his influence to see that the plan satisfied the American bankers who would have to sponsor it. The pertinent correspondence is in *Foreign Relations*, 1924, II, 30, *et seq.*

trouble which the International Bank for Reconstruction and Development had, a few years ago while preparing for its first bond issue.

In view of the demand for the Dawes Loan, it is not to be wondered that circulars of other German loans soon filled the mailboxes of prospects. They were, during the coming years, offered the choice of the promises to pay of the German Federal Government, German states and cities, the banks and mortgage companies, the railways, steamship lines, and canal companies, of the iron and steel corporations, and of the great electrical and chemical plants, for mines and automobile factories, chain stores and motion picture chains, and for religious institutions. Our financial mechanism was busily creating future targets for our bombers. Some were easier to set up than to knock down.

By the end of 1924 the State Department grew worried about the fact that German states and cities were pledging to the payment of the bonds issued here certain assets and revenues to which the claimants of reparations had first right. Article 248 of the Treaty of Versailles created " a first charge upon all the assets and revenues of the German Empire and its constituent states " in favor of reparation and other treaty payments, subject to such exceptions as the Reparation Commission might approve. The State Department began to call this clause to the attention of the bankers both verbally and in writing. The banking syndicates hastened to reply. They were assured, they said, by Owen D. Young that there would be no trouble from that angle; therefore they thought it would serve no practical purpose to make specific reference to this aspect of the loan offering in their circulars. The American Government merely reserved its position and let the matter go at that.

Shortly afterwards, the German authorities, activated by Schacht, then the head of the Reichsbank, reached the conclusion that the borrowing of German cities and provinces was wasteful. The Federal Government set up a form of control whereby German provinces and cities were required to get permission before floating foreign loans. The State Department, thereafter, when consulted by the bankers, always asked whether the necessary assent had been secured. But it did not always insist on a conclusive answer.

In the course of the next three years (1925-27) S. Parker Gilbert, the Agent for Reparations, became much worried by the size and laxity of the lending to Germany. He began to give public and private scoldings, and to warn the bankers and the State Department. So did our Ambassador in Berlin, Schurman. Thereafter the official responses to the bankers became two pages long and full of cautions. I will not repeat them in detail for the letters usually ended as follows:

While the foregoing considerations involve questions of business risk, and while the Department does not in any case pass upon the merits of foreign loans as business propositions, it is unwilling, in view of the uncertainties of the situation, to allow the matter to pass without calling the foregoing considerations to your attention. In reply to your inquiry, however, I beg to state that there appear to be no questions of Government policy involved which would justify the Department in offering objection to the loan in question.[2]

The financing went on. It slowed up a little after the State Department warned the German Government in 1927 that if it did not keep strict check on borrowing here, the American Government would have to do so.[3]

[2] For examples of these warnings, see *Foreign Relations*, 1925, II, 176, *et seq.*; 1926, II, 201, *et seq.*; 1927, II, 727, *et seq.*; 1928, II, 898, *et seq.*

[3] This warning was occasioned by a contemplated loan to the State of Prussia in September, 1927.—*Ibid.*, 1927, II, 728-29.

But the check was neither strict nor constant. The next great reparations crisis was weathered with the help of another large international loan for the German Government — the so-called "Young Loan." Secretary Mellon endorsed it and remarked (June 25, 1930) that "[it] marks a fundamental change in the situation. It is in itself an act of confidence in Germany's good faith and financial integrity and it calls for a corresponding effort on the German side." At the same time he reiterated that the obligation of our former allies to pay the war debts due to the United States was unconnected with the payment of reparations by Germany.

Still it is not easy to understand how the National City Company could tell its clients (Circular of June 14, 1930): "It is reasonable to believe that the new loan, which initiated many investors to the purchases of German securities, marks the beginning of a widening demand for German bonds, both in this country and abroad. And the present, therefore, would seem to be an opportune time for their purchase."

Comment on this experience is almost superfluous. We showed ignorance of both finance and politics.

It should have been evident that the taped structure of war debts, reparations, and foreign lending to Germany would at some near time break. What the State Department did to constrain the lending to Germany and bring about international monetary order had to be done in the face of objections to going as far as it did. Congress—with a majority of popular support—was unyielding on the war debts. Back of the financial mistake was the error of our tariff policy—supported by decades of belief that American prosperity rested on "protection."

When the smash came it was heard round the world. The German Republic fell into the ruins and Hitler rose from them.

It may be argued that the extension of American aid to
Germany was, in root and principle, a blunder—certain to
turn out wrong. Or (and this I think the more real view
of the alternative before us), that it would have been
reckless to refuse to assist German recovery after the war;
that the mistake lay in our failure (a failure not only of
the United States but also of its allies and associates)
before, while, and *after* we were doing so, to take the
measures that might have prevented our aid from ending
so badly. We did not do enough after the end of the war
to chasten and reform the German people. Or later to
encourage the Republic; or after Hitler appeared to demand his head; or to give enough support to those nations
that resisted him.

This case more than any other shows how unreliable
the outcome of foreign financing can be in a political fog,
how essential it is to have a clear and strong political and
military foundation for each of the main segments of our
economic program.

2

Both before and after our recognition of the Union of
Socialist Soviet Republics, the State Department discouraged all public credit operations for the Soviet Union.

As stated by Secretary Hughes (March 21, 1923) the
American Government thought that "not only would it
be a mistaken policy to give encouragement to repudiation
and confiscation, but it is also important to remember
that there should be no encouragement to the effort of
those Soviet authorities to visit upon other people the
disasters which have overwhelmed the Russian people."
This view was reiterated whenever the question arose—
most bluntly in the press release issued in February 1928,
"The Department does not view with favor financial

arrangements designed to facilitate in any way the sale of Soviet bonds in the United States."

The Soviet Union had decreed (January 21, 1918) that ". . . unconditionally, and without any exceptions, all foreign loans are annulled." This had been applied to the loans, about $187 million, which the American Government had made to the Kerensky regime, as well as to all private loans. The Soviet Union had also taken possession, without compensation, of various American owned enterprises in Russia. Neither persuasion nor the refusal to allow it to secure capital here, budged it to recognize old debts.

Even without official objection there would not have been much of a market in the United States for Soviet securities. But from time to time proposals emerged, as when one American banking syndicate wanted to sell Russian railroad bonds, and when another proposed to sell bonds of an American corporation which in turn would make a loan to the Soviet Union to build and equip steel plants. The most interesting of the rejected transactions was a deal sponsored by Harriman and Company in 1926 to loan $35 million (to be raised by a public issue of bonds) to a German export company, in order to finance exports from Germany to the Soviet Union. The Department made it clear that it would not view this financing with favor.[4]

The objection was not carried to the point of preventing the American banks from giving short-term credits to Russian state organizations to finance American exports, such as cotton. Nor to contracts whereby large American corporations like General Electric, General Motors, and the American Locomotive Company sold their products

[4] The pertinent correspondence is in *Foreign Relations, 1926,* II, pp. 906-10.

to Russian Government trusts on a credit basis. There was no interference with the customary type of business transaction or business credit.

During the twenties it was part of the doctrine of the Soviet Union that it would not plead for credit among the Capitalist states. Still the wish to open up the possibility of borrowing in this country was among the reasons why the Government of the Soviet Union sought recognition by us. But after the event it turned out that the Soviet Union would only make payment on old debts if it could borrow more, at once.

In brief, it would appear that official objection did not affect American political or economic relations with the Soviet Union in a vital way.

3

During the period of which I speak, American capital was welcome almost anywhere, for any purpose. In its exuberant tours of the world for things to do, the door was seldom closed. But here and there, where foreign groups possessed a prize which they did not want to share, entry was made hard.

In one such situation—the oil of the Middle East—the American Government took a determined interest; and did much more than it usually did to aid American capital to get the wanted chance. Much has been written about this long episode. But of one part, the contest which preceded the acquisition by American oil companies of a share in the oil of Mesopotamia, the story has still to be fully told.[5]

It is, I think, worth the telling for two reasons. First, because this contest opened the way for the extensive

[5] The main but by no means all the correspondence about this matter is printed in *Foreign Relations* in various volumes of the years 1920 to 1927.

operations which American capital are now conducting in Middle Eastern oil. Second, because it exemplifies the importance which the American Government attached at the time (and still attaches) to the principle named "the Open Door." [6]

This doctrine has been put to many uses by the American Government in the course of the past century. It has sometimes been a protection for small or weak countries threatened by political demands; sometimes a lever to crack open a foreclosed domain so that American interests could secure a share; sometimes a line of restraint on American enterprise; sometimes a shield behind which American productive strength could have full effect. It is at the heart of a conception which has been influential in the past conduct of American foreign policy: that the distribution of economic activity and opportunity in the world at large should be settled by competition — not politics.

But to return to the oil of Mesopotamia. At the end of World War I the American Government grew alarmed lest American oil supplies would soon fail to meet our needs and we should become vitally dependent on the

[6] We had insisted on writing it, at length and in all its aspects, into the Nine-Power Treaty of 1922, whereby all the powers with interests in the Pacific agreed upon the principles which were to govern their relations with China. In Article III of this Treaty the contracting parties other than China agreed that they would not seek or support their respective nationals in seeking " (a) any arrangement which might purport to establish in favor of their interests any general superiority of rights with respect to commercial or economic development in any designated region of China; (b) any such monopoly or preference as would deprive the nationals of any other Power of the right of undertaking any legitimate trade or industry in China, or of participating with the Chinese Government, or with any local authority, in any category of public enterprise, or which by reason of its scope, duration or geographical extent is calculated to frustrate the practical application of the principle of equal opportunity."

outside world. It was therefore eager for American oil
interests to search for and begin to produce oil abroad.
Its interest and attitude are well expressed in the opening
sentence of the diplomatic circular which on August 6,
1919, the State Department sent to its diplomatic and
consular officers. This read: "The vital importance of
securing adequate supplies of mineral oil both for the
present and future needs of the United States has been
forcibly brought to the attention of the Department."

Not too much was known then of the exact location or
extent of the oil deposits in the region between the Levant
coast and the Persian Gulf. But the secret reports and
rumors conveyed sensational promise. The territory in
Asia which Turkey had lost to the allies during and after
the war was supposed to contain great fields. Britain and
France had reached an agreement, whereby this territory
was to be allocated between three mandates under the
League of Nations—currently named Mesopotamia, Palestine, and Syria. Britain was to be the mandatory power
for Mesopotamia and Palestine, and France for Syria.
The mandate for Mesopotamia was to include the former
Turkish provinces of Mosul and Bagdad. There, of all
places, oil was supposed to be.

Before the war British and German groups, aided by
their Foreign Offices, had for some years competed with
one another to secure a concession from the Turkish Government for the oil of Mesopotamia. They had blocked
one another. Then, in early 1914, the British and German
Governments as part of an accord on spheres of influence
had induced the competing financial and oil interests to
combine. In March they had consolidated in a single
company which took the name of the Turkish Petroleum
Company (the name previously borne by the British con-
testant for the concession). In this the Anglo-Persian Oil

Company, controlled by the British Government, was to have a half interest; the Dutch Shell, a quarter interest; and the German group, a quarter interest. The Grand Vizier of Turkey had promised to grant this company a concession to develop the oil in the provinces of Mosul and Bagdad, but with certain provisos which were still under discussion when the war broke out and Turkey became an enemy. The Turkish Parliament had not ratified the grant. But after the war the British Government firmly argued that it was none the less valid, and that the question of who was to develop the oil of Mesopotamia was settled.[7]

In April, 1920, the British and French Governments and oil interests reached a capacious bargain—known as the San Remo Agreement—in regard to their respective rights in many areas—including Mesopotamia. The French were accorded the quarter share of output or ownership of the Turkish Petroleum Company which had belonged to the Germans. In return, the French agreed that this company should be under permanent British control, and to allow the construction of pipe lines from Mesopotamia and Persia through the French sphere of influence in Syria to a port or ports on the Eastern Mediterranean.[8]

The American Government protested all features of this settlement. It challenged the policies of the mandatory states, denied the validity of the concession of the Turkish Petroleum Company, and denounced the San Remo accord. In a series of notes to the British Govern-

[7] For an authoritative account of the early history of this concession and a more thorough analysis of the basis of the British claim, see the article by Edward Mead Earle in the *Political Science Quarterly* of June, 1924, " The Turkish Petroleum Company — A Study in Oleaginous Diplomacy."

[8] The text of the San Remo Oil Agreement is given in *Parliamentary Papers. Command*, 675 (1920).

ment (of which the most blunt was that of November 20, 1920) it asserted that American interests were entitled to equal opportunity within the mandates; that the claim alleged in behalf of the Turkish Petroleum Company would not be recognized; and that the San Remo bargain was unfair and illegitimate. "The reported resources of Mesopotamia," this note flatly declared, "have interested public opinion in the United States as a potential subject of international strife."[9]

Meanwhile the Government had urged the American oil companies to make a place for themselves in the Middle East. The Standard Oil Company of New Jersey took the lead. In November, 1921, it informed Secretary Hughes that a group of seven companies wanted the chance to examine the oil deposits in the Middle East and to develop them if the evidence warranted. Hughes welcomed this initiative. He promised to give them such help as he could. But he explained that the British Government was still taking the position that it could not allow any oil exploration in Mesopotamia by anyone until the military emergency ended. The explanation was mistrusted, for it was known that British geologists, in close touch with the Anglo-Persian Oil Company, had explored the region.[10]

The opposition of the American Government began to

[9] Mr. Colby to Lord Curzon, November 20, 1920: "Correspondence between His Majesty's Government and the United States Ambassdor respecting Economic Rights in Mandated Territories," *ibid.*, 675 (1921).

[10] Mr. E. L. De Golyer in his interesting account of American attempts to secure oil rights in the Middle East, tells of the geological investigation of the oil fields in Mesopotamia conducted by E. H. Pascoe, a geologist attached to the Geological Survey of India. He observes that a similar investigation of the oil fields of Persia made by the same expert in 1913-14, had preceded the purchase by the British Government of shares in the Anglo-Persian Oil Company.— See his essay, "The Oil Fields of the Middle East," printed in *Problems of the Middle East* (New York University, 1947).

take effect. This was in part because Britain and France were having to deal with the new and assertive Nationalist Turkish Government which was rising from the ruins of the Ottoman Empire. This had driven the Greeks backward and destroyed the basis for the Treaty of Sevres. It also began to dispute the inclusion of the province of Mosul in the Mandate of Mesopotamia. The chance appeared that the American Government might support the Turkish claims. In any case the British and French oil interests began to make place for the American. In June, 1922, the partners in the Turkish Petroleum Company offered the American oil group a 20 per cent participation in their concession. To grant this the share of the Anglo-Persian Company was to be reduced to 40 per cent, that of the Dutch Shell to 20 per cent and that of the French group to 20 per cent.

Secretary Hughes was consulted as to whether such an accord would be deemed by the American Government consonant with the principle of the open door. Hughes found himself pinched between the wish to have Americans acquire a share of Middle Eastern oil and dislike for an arrangement that might turn out to be a monopoly. He answered the group by saying that the Government did not want to be impractical; and that therefore it would not object on various conditions. These were (a) that the American group would take in any other American oil companies that might want to join it; (b) that the claims of the Turkish Petroleum Company should not be' recognized except after impartial determination as suggested by the American Government; and (c) that the combined groups should not monopolize the oil resources of the region.

The project of combination was next held up by differences between the oil groups. The American companies asked for more than 20 per cent. The French, who were no longer working hand in hand with the British, were ready to support this American request provided that the French share would be the same as the American. While, in contrast, the Dutch Shell Company did not want to see its part reduced from 25 to 20 per cent to make place for the Americans; it thought that all of the share to be given the Americans, or almost all, should be passed over by the Anglo-Persian Company. While this issue was still being discussed, the American Government continued to raise the troubling question as to whether the combination were about to acquire a monopoly which would vitiate the idea of the open door.

But during the second half of 1922 amiable adjustments of these questions seemed in sight. The European powers were meeting at Lausanne to write a new peace treaty with Turkey. They had to reckon not only with Turkey but with the lurking opposition of the American Government. Lord Curzon, the Secretary of State for Foreign Affairs, announced that Great Britain would give up the San Remo Accord and support the principle of the open door.

The Anglo-Persian Oil Company matched this statement with a new proposal. It offered to increase both the American and French shares to 24 per cent and accept that much smaller share for itself. But on these three conditions: first, that it would receive a 10 per cent royalty on all the oil produced; second, that the State Department would not keep on questioning the validity of the concession of the Turkish Petroleum Company; and third, that the State Department would tell its observers at the Lausanne Conference that agreement had been reached along these lines and support this solution " to the exclusion of any other interest, American or otherwise." This third point reflected British concern lest after one American group had received a round share in the Turkish Petroleum Company other American rivals would appear. American oil companies—either those in the group or those outside it — might seek rights in Mesopotamia from the new Arab Government; the American Government might support them; and then the Turkish Petroleum Company might find its position much impaired.

Secretary Hughes was reserved about this new offer. He repeated his opinion that a new grant should be sought before the company tried to engage in oil development. He would not promise to abstain from aiding other American interests that might want to enter the area. This answer forced a search for new terms of a bargain.

While the search was on, as always happens in the Middle East, a new element entered. At the turn of the century President Theodore Roosevelt had sent a young American admiral on a battleship to Turkey on a mission of protection and persuasion. Admiral Colby M. Chester had made influential friends in Turkey and became enthused about what could be done in that country by American capital and enterprise. Before the war, interests whom he enlisted had gone far in discussion with the Turkish Government of various schemes. But because of the upsets in the Turkish Government, the Balkan wars, and British and German rivalry, none had been completed. During the years of World War I Chester had kept in touch with the rulers of Turkey.

Now in April, 1923, shortly before the powers met for a second time at Lausanne to try again to frame a peace with Turkey, the Government of that country granted the Chester group (which had named itself the Ottoman-American Development Company) one of the world's most remarkable concessions. This conveyed the right to build roads and railways the length and breadth of what was left of Turkey, to operate public utilities, to create a new capital at Ankara, to construct harbors in the Mediterranean and the Black Sea, and to develop the oil and mineral resources along the lines of the railways. The province of Mosul was included within the area of this grant. The Turkish Government, it may be safely surmised, knew that there was little chance that the Chester group would be able to carry out these projects. But it kept the competition alive and publicized the possibility.[11]

The British Government remained calm. But the French authorities grew excited, since some of the railway rights included in the Chester concession were already pledged to the French. The State Department gave the impression that it saw nothing in the Chester concession which would prevent it from lending diplomatic support, if it chose.

All this added to the confusion inside and outside the second Lausanne Conference as to who had or was to have the oil of Mosul. The British Government tried to persuade the Turkish Government to confirm the validity of the concession of the Turkish Petroleum Company in a protocol to the Treaty of Peace. The American Government directed its observer, Joseph C. Grew (at that time Minister to Turkey), to make clear that it was " unalterably opposed " to such action. It also protested directly to the British, French and Italian Governments and warned Ismet Pasha that if he accepted this provision Turkey could not expect American citizens to continue their interest in economic ventures in Turkey. Hughes main-

---

[11] The group was in fact, badly split in factions and had had barely enough funds to pay the cable bills. The State Department for a time was cool because of a suspicion that the Ottoman-American Company was controlled by Canadian interests. But in December, 1922, it had authorized the Acting High Commissioner at Constantinople (Dolbeare) " to give such diplomatic support as may be proper."

tained this opinion more or less against the wishes of the American oil group who by then thought themselves on the edge of a good bargain with the British and French groups.

In the upshot, the Peace Treaty was silent about Mosul oil. The question as to whether the province was to be included in Turkey or Iraq was referred to the Council of the League of Nations.[12]

By 1923 plans were under way to drop the mandate for Mesopotamia and turn the region—which became known as Iraq—over to an Arab government. In September the Turkish Petroleum Company applied to the Government of Iraq for an oil concession. This was to include not only Bagdad and Mosul provinces, but also Basra province.

Hughes was disturbed lest the requested grant also turn out to be a monopoly, contrary to the open-door idea. But his qualms were somewhat lessened by one new feature which at the initiative of the American group was to be written into the accord. The recipient was not to retain permanent control of the whole area under concession. It was to offer annually not less than twenty-four plots for competition " without distinction of nationality " to any responsible person who desired leases. The Government, subject to its rights of reasonable disapproval, was required to grant a lease to the highest bidder of each plot. Proceeds of the lease were to be paid over to the company.[13]

Hughes consulted President Coolidge as to whether to favor or oppose this new arrangement. He told Coolidge that he was afraid that if the American Government

[12] Article 4 of the Treaty of Lausanne. — *Parliamentary Papers. Command*, 1929. Treaty series No. 16, 1923.

[13] This is the form in which the accord finally appeared in Article 6 of the Concession granted by Iraq in March 14, 1925.

maintained too rigid a position the American group would drop out, and that the British and French would get the desired concession from Iraq anyhow and go ahead on their own. Thus he told the American group that he was ready to give American diplomatic support for the application of the Turkish Petroleum Company. But at the same time he took the chance to emphasize the prospect held out by the sublease provision, that other oil companies would be given a chance to share in the development of the oil fields of Iraq.

Thus the pattern of control was decided. But there were still loose lines and strands; and it took several more years of knitting to get them into pleasing place. The oil groups had to trade it out with an individual claimant, Gulbenkian, who had been useful in connection with the original grant. His wishes and those of the Americans crisscrossed on the question as to whether the participants were merely to divide control of the stock, or also the actual oil produced. The Iraq Government took exception to the subleasing provision. Some observers were of the opinion that the British Colonial Office might have aroused the mistrust of the new ruler of Iraq, Emir Feisal, as to the intent and effect of the arrangement.

Last but not least, the Turkish Government continued to maintain that Mosul was part of its territory—an issue over which the Council of the League of Nations lingered. There were some who found in this fact an explanation of why the American group did not hurry to close the deal. They might be waiting to see who would turn out to be the ruler of the province of Mosul. They could wait, for since first they had sought entry into the Middle East the oil situation had changed. Scarcity had turned into surplus. Large new reserves were in sight in Texas and in the Caribbean. There were no great profitable markets waiting for Middle Eastern oil.

In March, 1925, the new concession, issued by the Government of Iraq, was signed. The following December, after a decision of the Permanent Court of International Justice, the Council of the League of Nations awarded the province of Mosul to Iraq. The British and Turkish Governments reached an agreement. Turkey was to get 10 per cent of the revenue accruing to Iraq from oil during twenty-five years.

The British, American, and French groups finally reached an accord. The share allocated to the American group was 23¾ per cent, the same to the French, and 5 per cent to Mr. Gulbenkian. The Iraq Petroleum Company (by such changes of name the change of rulers is marked) is alone engaged in oil production in what was Mesopotamia. The provision for sublease, conceived to satisfy the principle of the open door, was not carried into effect. Because of disturbed conditions in Iraq in 1927-28, which also deterred the company from starting operations, it was agreed to postpone its application. Then when in 1931 a Revised Agreement was signed between Iraq and the Iraq Petroleum Company the provision was omitted.

American oil interests who were not in the Iraq group found in later years better chances elsewhere, particularly in the nearby Arab lands of Saudi Arabia, Bahrein, and Kuwait. In each of these, too, the State Department helped to gain admission.

Towards the end of World War II rivalry and dispute between British and American interests desirous of getting or producing oil in the Middle East again loomed up. But differences this time concerned the wish of American enterprises to rush forward with production and pipe lines, rather than concession rights. In 1943 the American Government, in emulation of the Anglo-Iranian Company, sought to become owner of the American oil properties in the region; and a year later it stepped forth with an offer to build a pipe line from the oil fields near the shores of the Persian Gulf to the Mediterranean. But both of these projects were soon dropped. Subsequently the American and British oil companies concerned reached an adjustment of interest, and what might be called a " harmonic rhythm," in their operations and plans. This may be now threatened by the wish and need of Britain to save dollars.

The tale of these later events is too long to tell on this occasion. So I leave it with the bare comment that the American investment in Middle Eastern oil—of which the dispute over the oil of Mosul was the prelude—is in course of becoming the largest venture of American private capital in foreign lands. Not only the largest; the one most likely to figure most often in the annals of our future diplomacy.

I end my citations of instances. Those given suffice, I hope, to show the range, chief traits, failures, and successes of this venture of the dollar in diplomacy. But for those who seek not only the story but the meaning, I shall try to draw conclusions.

CHAPTER IV

REFLECTIONS AND COMPARISONS

1

IT IS useful to attempt a rough summing up of this earlier experience in having the dollar be an important agent in our foreign affairs. Useful, that is, as a stimulant to reflection, not as a manual which exactly tells what we should or should not do in the future. We can learn by experience. But only by keeping clear, always, and at every point, the difference between the terms of each past situation and each of those that lie ahead. We all know of battles lost because the general conducted the fight in a way which was figured out in school as sure to have won some battle in the past. Some of the policies that proved sound the last time might be unpractical or foolish the next time. Some of the policies that proved faulty the last time might work well the next; while there are other mistakes, unnumbered, which wait for us. The past is a good tutor only to those who take full measure of the here and now, and perhaps I should add, the hereafter. The reader may recall Lord Bryce's comment [in his book The American Commonwealth] " . . . the chief practical use of history is to deliver us from plausible historical analogues."

As seen in the mirror of the present, these points about the earlier experience stand out:

1. The first proximate purposes which appealed to the Government were for a time achieved. American capital greatly helped the war damaged and dislocated world to

61

get back into working order. It alleviated much suffering
abroad. It induced production and employment at home.
It made far easier the transit from ruined currencies to
sound ones. It restored trade and augmented world supplies of food and raw materials. It buoyed up the opera-
tion of the capitalist system in Europe. Many countries
of South America and also of the British Commonwealth
were also helped to grow and gain.

2.   But these benefits were lost when depression spread.
The whole world, in greater or less degree, had become
dependent upon a continuance of a high level of economic
activity in the United States. Prices, debt structures,
trade flows all rested on the stimulus of our demand and
our investment. Both fell abruptly. Ever since, foreign
countries—especially those of the British Commonwealth
—have been afraid to rely too much on the stability of
our economic situation; and Soviet Communism has tried
to destroy faith in our value as an economic ally by pre-
dicting that we would repeat the tumble.

3.   A substantial fraction of our loans served merely
to enable foreign borrowers to pay older or other obligations. Thus, we supplied the means by which Germany
paid reparations, thereby indirectly supplying the means
whereby our Allies paid debts to the American Treasury
and interest on earlier loans made by private American
lenders.

4.   We failed sufficiently to increase our imports of
foreign goods. Hence the restored two-way stream of
trade never attained a healthy balance between ourselves
and the rest of the world. We oversold; the others under-
sold. Neither we nor they adjusted internal productive
arrangements to suit the debtor-creditor relation that was
being created; and this meant that the relation was easily
smashed.

5.   Our economic aid for a time offset the suppressive effects of the fears of war and deep social change in many countries of Europe. But after the depression set in, these returned in full force. In any case financial means and measures alone could not have genuinely dispelled these fears—derived from deep divisions between nations in Europe and the Far East, and from the rumbles of revolutionary change. Whether, if our program of economic leadership had been more sustained, and combined with full use of our political and military influence, the world could have been tranquillized, I do not know. But I think the chance was within grasp.

6.   After Hitler emerged in Germany, there was urgent cause for a great campaign to make the dollar tell. But instead, it went into retirement, gave up the field. Private American capital was hard hit and scared. The American Government came to its rescue, but did not take over the sustaining task. It was deeply concerned and wanted to be helpful. But it lacked the boldness and the support to use American resources and strength to prevent the crisis from becoming a catastrophe.

We should have begun at once, and on a greater scale, to supply the more peacefully inclined countries with the dollars they needed to become strong. Ten billion during the thirties for the British Empire and Commonwealth, France, China, and the other opponents of Germany and Japan might have made the difference between peace and war. But only, if we had been ready to back the dollar with our diplomacy, and, if essential, by arms.

7.   Failing in these respects, it worked out that the political results of our venture in dollar diplomacy were, in a word, "lamentable."

The American people had a hazy, lazy faith that their loans and investments would spread American ideals, foster good will and trust between ourselves and foreign countries, encourage disarmament, and bring reconciliation and peace. The soldiers and sailors had done their part, the dollar was counted on to carry on their work. It was regarded as a kind of universal balm, good for all peoples and all ailments. The American Executive shared this attitude, though wistfully aware that the mien and response of some foreign nations was not all that could be wished. The American Congress, led by Senators Borah, Lodge, and Johnson, was suspicious of the whole activity, as a snare of the international bankers and foreign politicians.

It need hardly be said that the hopes were disappointed. A few political and national differences were adjusted but not the deeper ones: the pause in competitive armaments was short: a new group of aggressors broke through the weak wall of treaties; and war came again, and we were forced to join it. Contrary to wish and intention, part of our lending enabled the aggressors to grow strong.

This is not to suggest that the failure of American foreign policy between the wars was due, in significant measure, to mistakes in the way the dollar was used. The main line of consequence is the other way about. We mistook the good that could have come under the circumstances from sending our capital abroad; and then spoiled the chance of doing any lasting good because other branches of our foreign policy were so defective. After our attempt to organize peace on the basis of treaties failed, we strove to be neutral, isolated, and unoffending. We remained out of the League of Nations. We refused to join in any systematized effort to deter the aggressive thrusts of Germany, Italy and Japan. We failed to maintain armed forces large enough to gain respect for our wishes. And while the world went on its way—the dollar, chaperon of the first decade, discouraged, stayed at home.

At best it is hard to foresee the ultimate political results of providing capital to many of the foreign nations which seek it. Regimes come and go. Alliances form, break, and reform. Loyalties shift. The relative strength of nations changes over a period of time. Thus, even when a country's foreign policy is well reckoned and clear, the task of directing its foreign investment over a span, say of three decades, is something like pinning the tail on the donkey, blindfolded. When the foreign policy is neither adequate nor clear, it is not possible to know even where the donkey is. That was the case in the two decades between the wars.

In another political purpose we had some successes, some failures. It was hoped that with economic improvement foreign nations would adopt a form of political system resembling our own. We looked for the emergence of constitutional government, under which individual freedom and justice would be respected. In some places our financial aid stimulated progress in the desired direction. It prevented certain bad governments from obtaining or keeping office in Latin American countries, and assisted better ones to succeed. It helped some democracies of certain European countries to meet threatening crises. It made it possible for a democratic form of government to operate for a time in Germany against intense opposition. But, on the other hand, it sustained some governments hostile to democracy—as, for example, Mussolini's rule in Italy.

Let me quit this review of the past by summarizing the experience in another way. It turned out that the dollar, *in the amounts in which it was made available and linked to an inadequate foreign policy*, could not counteract or control certain basic and historic forces. It could not, for example, change the low birth rate in France, which made that country yielding, or the high birth rate in Japan, which made that country crowded and restless. Nor could it wipe out that sense of frustration, envy, and hatred, which again turned Germany into an aggressor; nor bring back those able young men that Britain lost in World War I, to guide the British Empire and direct British industry. Nor could it make the Chinese Government unified, competent, and progressive. Nor, to conclude the list of examples, could it have caused the Soviet Union to cease striving for world-wide revolution.

Whether we should have had more success had the dollar investment been steadier and greater, had there been no depression, had our foreign policy been different, had our Army, Navy and Air Force been made as great as the greatest, I do not know. But I am inclined to think so; to think that the experience was not a fair test of the contribution that the dollar can make to the permanent improvement of life among nations.

2

The foregoing is, I realize, a sober, if not somber, preface to any remarks about that larger venture in dollar diplomacy in which we are now engaged. Let it be so. We have been in danger of yielding again to the rhetoric of unmeasured hope; and thus of being depressed and impatient because the recipients of our capital do not fully live up to the image of our hope. We are now distressed because results have not matched the promises which the sponsors attached to certain of our activities-in-aid: the struggle of Britain, though much helped, quickly to achieve international solvency, the collapse of the Chiang Kai-shek regime in China, despite our support, the instability and incompetence of the governments in some of the Latin American lands in which we had invested heavily, the threatened economic failure in the Philippines.

Other lags and frustrations of our purposes are to be expected; often enough to cause us to smile at the forecasts of these economists who, heedless of the hob that passions, interests, social divisions and hatreds and national boundary lines can play with charts of potential productivity, wrote as though investment could cure all the ills to which nations are subject. To cause us also to test with salt such phrases as those found in President Truman's first explanation of the plan to provide technical assistance to foreign countries (the so-called "Point 4"). "This was," he said in part, ". . . to help create the conditions that will lead eventually to personal freedom and happiness for all mankind. *Ad astra per aspera*!

Such visions are not wholesome in this rough world; they are sure to be followed by attacks of green sickness. Nor are they necessary to give meaning to, or justify our present program of foreign lending and giving.

That emerged from reasons which were compelling— and remain so. The need of other countries for aid in recuperating from the strains of the past decade, and in adjusting their social systems to the new conceptions and pressures, has been imperative. The danger that if left unaided many of the states of Western Europe and of the Far East would be conquered by communism or suffer prolonged civil war has been and remains sharp and close. Had we again refused to take heed of this situation, again refused to test what could be done by our economic strength, it would have been a foolish invitation to disaster.

The dollar has already served—and served well—as a buffer against the extension of chaos and communism. Being thus inspired, the nature and size of our program (or, the same thing another way, the diplomacy of the dollar) has been settled by blows struck from without rather than by theory or free choice. We have tried hard and worthily to get off the plane of necessity, and on to one of orderly economic and political programming and judging. We are on our way there if war does not engulf the world.

This means that not many fixed lines or dimensions are to be found—thus far—in this current venture of ours in the diplomacy of the dollar. A clear basic idea exists, I believe, of what we are trying to achieve. But there will be, as there have been, many changes in judgment as to what must be done, or should be done, and how to do it. And many future barters with expediency; and many mean misjudgments of our motives and desires.

The brief span of this volume admits no more than a skeleton summary of this second experience — to date. But a few comments may help to tie past and present together in our thoughts.

All but a small fraction of the sums which we have lent or given this time to foreign countries have come out of the public purse, or have been backed by a Government guarantee. Here and there private capital has judged some foreign opportunity safe and attractive enough to undertake on its own—as in Canada and in some Latin American countries, the gold and copper mines of Africa, and the oil fields of the Middle East. But most seekers of dollars have not been able to offer either security or good chances of profit. The level of taxes here and abroad has been another deterrent. The burden, thus, of providing dollars, where national interest or purpose required, has fallen upon the Government — which means upon the citizen. It may well be wise and feasible from now on to do more by insuring private American ventures against loss, and less by direct Government action.

We were slow to recognize the full extent of the need of giving economic aid to the outside world, if it were not to be a sea of everlasting trouble. Our first impulse, as after the end of World War I, was to tell our allies that the war was over and that they should hustle to stand on their own feet. Hence the abrupt ending of Lend Lease aid.

Then when it became evident that much of the Western world could not get along without further help, we tried to meet the need by carefully measured loans. The biggest of these—the one made to Britain—was too small. In one respect its terms were too demanding: we forced Britain to make a premature and costly experiment in convertibility. In another respect its terms were careless: we failed to think out more thoroughly how the proceeds could best be used.

Our foreign financial outlay during those first postwar years (1945-47) did not have its due restorative effect. In part, this was because we (and our Allies) lost control over the postwar settlement of Europe and Asia. The United Nations turned out to be veto-bound. And as our military force declined, our authority ebbed away.

Then came the harsh winter and summer droughts of 1947, and it seemed as though we had the job all still to do. Many countries found themselves even less able than before to buy from us products essential to maintain their way of life and sustain their economies. The Soviet Union and the Communist elements everywhere intensified their attack upon democratic societies. They counted on misery, discontent, and fright to reduce all Europe and Asia to submission.

We revised our estimates, and called the dollar to the fore again. It was perceived that it would not be enough merely to continue the battle for recovery with the restrained and conventional tactics thus far used. We began to search for a program that by enlisting the economic energies of all the states of Europe in a cooperative effort might point the way also to new political understandings.

This was the original conception of ECA, the grand design of dollar diplomacy. We offered the whole of Europe more aid than ever, but said at the same time: Will you not all work together with us so that we may be reasonably sure, ten or twenty years hence, our dollars will have served a healing cause and brought lasting benefit? And also that our contribution to recovery will be multiplied because individuals and nations will again feel secure enough to engage their energies and fortunes fully in production and trade; and thus each become strong enough to do without us? The rejection by the Soviet Union of this bid for cooperation forced a deep change in this design.

At present our program has six parts, deemed supplementary to one another:

1. Through ECA we are providing dollars to eighteen countries of Western Europe to enable them to secure essential imports, while adjusting their production and trade so as to enable to manage presently without aid.

2. Through ECA and direct appropriations we have granted many countries in the Pacific—particularly the Philippines, the Dutch East Indies, Indo-China—substantial sums to restore war damaged economies and improve their condition.

3. Through ECA and direct appropriations we are helping to restore the economies of beaten former enemies—Germany and Japan —so that they will be able to satisfy their essential needs by their own efforts.

4. Through the Import-Export Bank and International Bank for Reconstruction and Development we are providing the means by which countries, outside of the main combat area of the last war, can add to their industry and improve their agriculture and use of their natural resources.

5. We have been sustaining, against the threat of invasion, the armed forces of Greece, Turkey and Iran, while also assisting them to return to peacetime economic conditions. Support of a similar kind, though smaller and less direct, is being given to Tito's regime in Yugoslavia, in its struggle against Moscow.

6. Under the approved, but not yet going program, we are planning to provide more technical aid and advice to foreign countries than ever before.

All these efforts are conjoined with an extensive program of military aid. If we fail to invigorate the friendly parts of the world and hold them together it will not be for want of trying. All parts of this vast and varied program may be said to have the same main general purpose: to aid all countries outside of the Soviet sphere to achieve an orderly, free, secure, and independent life—in the belief that they then will be stable friends and allies. But listen to what the Soviet Government says about it—through the mouth of Malenkov, at the last anniversary celebration of the 1917 Revolution, November 6, 1949:

It is nothing more nor less than a matter of converting the whole world into a colony of the American imperialists, of reducing sovereign peoples to the position of slaves.

Such an interpretation expresses the enmity which gives primary impetus to the program at present; namely, to strengthen other countries so that communism shall be rejected inside and resisted outside. This means that our strategy in the use of the dollar — for the time being at least — will be complex, variable and somewhat warped: that it cannot closely fit our desires, or our estimates of what would produce the greatest economic benefit, or of justice between recipients. But this hostility is apt to make us more determined and bold in the use of our economic strength, and more patient in enduring the cost and the vexations.

And determination and patience in full measure will be needed, since this field of activity will remain one of trial and error. It is impossible to foresee the future turns in conduct and allegiance of each of the foreign countries to whom we are providing dollars, or the future changes in their relations with one another. It is hard to know in some situations whether we may be making a friend or nourishing a viper. I hardly need illustrate. We are greatly helping to restore Western Germany. Who can be sure what its ultimate political allegiance will be? We have financed Italy, sustained Trieste, and are now beginning to support Yugoslavia. Will the dispute between these two countries be composed, or will it some day bring about war? We are helping in one way or another most of the small Arab states and also the state of Israel. Will they live in peace with one another? Will the Marshall Plan combination stand up effectively in case of a war crisis with the Soviet Union? Who can tell whether or not we will be able so to control events, that the answers to such riddles of the future as these will give us satisfaction, not grief?

But we are right to risk much on the faith that economic improvement, widely-shared and achieved by joint effort, will make it more likely that the nations outside of the Soviet sphere will hold together, adjust their differences; and that at some time the Soviet Union will suspend, if not renounce, its struggle for world domination. Right to venture the dollars we are giving, right to venture more.

But, to repeat, no matter how many dollars we risk, and how great the foresight with which we direct their use, no one can be sure of the result. For it will depend so largely on forces and decisions of others beyond our control. Some of the societies and countries we are aiding may fall apart anyhow. The international combination we are leading may be riven by dissension or prove too weak. The Soviet Union may provoke war. These are chances that cannot be wholly eliminated by the most vigorous use of the dollar, and most skilled conduct of other sections of our foreign policy. But the quality of our own performance may determine whether the chance of realizing our aims is good or poor.

The earlier experience which I have reviewed provides the material, I think, for defining some of the essentials for success.

First, it is essential to maintain a stable and high level of economic activity within the United States. And in this connection it is well to bear in mind that the program of dollar aid, itself, keeps our internal economic situation distorted. We should be making advance provision to adjust and redistribute our economic activities so as to be able to avoid depression, if and as we find it wise to reduce our program of foreign dollar expenditure.

Second, it is essential to convince other nations that we are not animated solely by a wish for our national safety or narrow advantage, or wedded to empty material aims. We must endow material progress with meaning outside and beyond itself. I do not mean — by coating it with a sheen of advertising. I mean by showing in action the best qualities that are in us; so that we appear as porters of a good civilization, a friendly, just, and secure one — not merely as masters of mass production. That is what we must stand for in the world's eyes—as we come bringing gifts.

Third (or perhaps I should put it first), as long as there is no reliable political accord with the Soviet Union, and no agreement about the use of atomic weapons, we must maintain a military force strong enough to meet the Soviet Union in war. And also proceed urgently with plans under way for combining our strength with that of Western Europe. We have lagged badly in both tasks.

Fourth, it is essential to maintain constant and coherent connection between the diplomacy of the dollar, our domestic and foreign economic policies, our political relations, and our military effort. Each must serve the others and be adjusted to the others.

The changes in our foreign economic policies have been rapid and marked. To the end that the countries assisted by the dollar may become able to sustain themselves through trade we have reduced our tariffs. We have accepted without complaint devaluations of foreign currencies which may displace our trade in foreign markets. We have sent industrial and technical missions throughout the world to aid foreign countries to improve their methods of production and, thereby, their chance of competing with us. In sum, our attempt to use our capital as an agent to transform the world's trading pattern is generous and vigorous. But still, to interject a doubt amid the praise, it will probably turn out we have put the world too heavily in our debt; that future payments due on much of the sums that have been given the formal financial guise of loans and investments cannot be made in full— without undoing what we are trying to do. The annual debt service solely on loans already made by the American government to foreign governments will be in 1952 about 500 million dollars.

Of the new departures in our foreign political policy— in line with our program of foreign aid—I have little need to speak. They are displayed in the active part we take in the United Nations Organization, the North Atlantic Treaty, the Organization of American States, and the Mutual Defense Assistance Program.

In all these and other directions we are recognizing the need to concert all branches of our foreign operations. This —without removing the diplomacy of the dollar from the realm of the unpredictable—gives it a justifying chance.

But we have still, I think, to improve our ways. We still slip at times into the same kind of impulsive thinking and hasty talking that marked the first venture. Let me illustrate by commenting on some of the conceptions about the ECA program that were current not long ago.

The idea was widely advanced that the program—in contrast, say, to our military program—*must* be a temporary or transient one; that no matter what, it *must* be brought to a quick end of our own choosing. This attitude was reflected in such impatient comments as that what we are after now is to " get Europe off our backs." This remark contains a strong strain of sound purpose. We are right in wanting the funds that we supply to be so used as to end the need for continued assistance. But will not that depend in part on what political assignments we expect Western Europe to carry out? Or how much of a part we expect them to bear in a combined military program? Such official slang is too simple for the situation; and it may create a troublesome basis for future decisions.

Again, take the abrupt turns in some of our ideas about what we expect of the countries receiving aid from us. At the start of the ECA we asked each participating country to come forward with its own national statement of how it proposed to balance its accounts with the outside world, and how much it needed to do so. They and we reviewed these estimates, changed and reduced them. But the program was essentially one of support of national systems, and it contemplated expansion of production in many fields — such as food and steel — heedless of comparative costs between the foreign countries concerned. The condition that first of all we laid down *then* was that each, as soon as it could, should observe the rule of equality of treatment in the economic field. Each country was to accord *every* other, *including the United States*, the same terms—no better, no worse—in matters of tariffs, quotas, exchange controls and the like. Non-discrimina-

tory, multilateral trade was the slogan — universal and
undefiled. Free convertibility of currencies was the
method; universal competition the ideal. In this cause we
lectured the world until we were hoarse with indignation.

But then it turned out that it was wiser to want something quite different of the countries of Western Europe.
We have been urging them, in phrases that sounded like
a threat to end our aid if they did not conform, to
"integrate" their economies. This could mean any one of
several things: that they should form a complete economic
(and perhaps political) union; or merely that they should
move towards free trade and free convertibility of currencies among themselves; or that various basic industries
like steel, coal, chemicals be combined into regional units.

Should we not have taken more care to be sure that
we were asking what it was feasible to ask, before issuing
what sounded at first like an ultimatum? Should we not
have estimated more thoroughly the tensions that might
result from a too drastic attempt to satisfy our wishes?
Who has yet ascertained, for example, how any plan of
integration, put abruptly into effect, would affect the
struggle against communism in certain countries? How
it would affect the relative power of German heavy industries? Whether it would bring about a location of industry
within the Western European area, that fits the joint
military program? How should economic integration be
timed to fit steps towards political or military integration?

Again, I would remark that the idea is of merit. All of
the members of OEEC would gain by freeing trade and
financial transactions among themselves, and the burden
upon us would be reduced. But obviously this is a matter
for method and measure, not for ultimatums.

It is time to conclude. What can I offer as grist or gist:
that our diplomacy of the dollar must be large and sus-

tained enough to effect our ends; that in the course of it we will meet many lags and failures, all kinds and often; that it must be kept in close accord with all other branches and phases of our foreign policy; and that the ultimate justification lies not in the material sphere, but in the hope that it will bring protection to all, and make life between nations less savage, maybe even friendly and just?

The outcome will, of course, depend not only on us but on each of the countries with whom we are trying to work. As tersely stated by Secretary of State Dean Acheson:

> We can help greatly those who are doing their utmost to succeed by their own efforts. We cannot direct or control; we cannot make a world, as God did, out of chaos.

It falls upon each of the others to put its house in order; to recognize that it cannot stand out alone; and to prove its capacity to survive as a free and cooperative nation. Our aid and leadership cannot take the place of their effort, but it can reward their effort with success.

INDEX

Acheson, Dean, Secretary of State, 77

Allied Chemical and Dye Company, 32

American Locomative Company, 47

Anglo-Iranian Oil Company see Anglo-Persian Oil Company

Anglo-Persion Oil Company, 50, 52-54, 59

Argentina, Government of, 30

Armaments, loans for, 19-20, 30-31

Austria, Government of, 39, 41

Bagdad Province, oil in, 50, 51, 57

Bahrein, oil in, 59

Bank of England, 4, 40

Belgium, Government of, 4, 20, 24

Bolivia, Government of, 31

Borah, Senator William H., 25, 64

Brazil, Coffee Institute of, 31

Bryce, Lord, 61

Buget deficits, loans to meet, 19, 32-33

Canada, Government of, 23, 28, 68

Central America, American loan policies in that region, 2, 9, 25-29

Chang Tso-lin, 37

Chase National Bank, 27

Chester, Admiral Colby M., 55-56

Chiang Kai-shek, 66

Chili, Government of, 30

China, Government of, 33, 37, 38, 49, 63, 66

China, North, 34

Clementel, Etienne, French Minister of Finance, 21, 22 n.

Colby, Bainbridge, Secretary of State, 52

Communists, 41

Coolidge, Calvin, President of the United States, 6, 29, 36, 57

Cotton, Joseph C., 13, 18

Cuba, Government of, 27

Curzon, Lord, 52 n., 54

Czechoslovakia, Government of, 24, 33

Dawes, Charles, General 42 n.

Dawes Loan, 40, 42, 43

Dawes Plan, 21, 41, 42

De Golyer, E. L., 52 n.

Dolbeare, Frederick, 56 n.

Dutch Shell Company, 51, 53-54

Earle, Edward Mead, 51 n.

ECA (Economic Cooperation Arministration) 70, 75

Federal Reserve Sytem, 4

Feisal, Emir, 58

Foreign Debt Commission, American World War, 22

France, Government of, 4, 20, 21, 22, 23, 24, 34, 41, 50-51, 53-54, 56-59, 63, 65

General Electric Company, 47

General Motors Corporation, 47

Germany, Government of, 21, 31, 33, 50, 55, 64-66; supervision of loans to, 12, 39-46

Gilbert, S. Parker, 44

Glass, Senator Carter, 12

Great Britain, Government of, 34, 41, 42 n., 50-60, 63, 66, 69

Greece, 20, 24, 53, 70

Grew, Joseph C., Minister to Turkey, 56

Guatemala, Government of, 28

Gulbenkian, Calouste, 58-59

Haiti, Government of, 9, 27; National Bank of, 28 n.

Harding, Warren G., President of the United States, 6, 7, 10, 11

Harriman and Company, 47

Harrison, Leland, vi

Herrick, Myron T., Ambassador to France, 21 n., 22 n.

Hitler, Adolf, 45, 46, 63

Holland, Government of, 4, 23

Honduras, Government of, 28

Hoover, Herbert, President of the United States, 6; Secretary of Commerce, 7, 8, 11, 18

Hughes, Charles Evans, Secretary of State, 6, 7, 8, 9, 10-11, 26, 34, 40, 42, 46, 52, 53, 55-57

Hungary, Government of, 39, 41

Import-Export Bank, 70